B. Chirva

# FOOTBALL
## Learning the basic elements of zonal pressing tactics

2014

УДК 796 332
Ч 64

Ч 64 **Chirva B.** Football. Learning the basic elements of zonal pressing tactics. – Moscow, 2014. – 214 c.

ISBN 978-5-98724-083-0

This book presents training method of basic elements of zonal pressing tactics.

Highlighted is a brief description of defensive actions in typical local situation with participation of one and two defending players during the zonal pressing.

Exercises for learning technique and raising the speed of actions performed during the zonal pressing, and acquisition of basic elements of zonal pressing tactics are suggested.

The book's materials are designed for coaches working in professional football teams and youth football.

УДК 796 332
Ч 64

ISBN 978-5-98724-186-8

# CONTENTS

# INTRODUCTION

At the turn of 21 century there was transition from man to man marking and libero to the zonal method of building of defending actions, which is due to different efficiency of one or another defensive play tactics.

At the modern stage of football development the zonal method of defense has come up with a new content which consists in its conversion into zonal pressing.

Zonal pressing is understood to be dynamic and powerful pressure on a player from the attacking team, who tries to take possession of the ball or already possessing it, put by players from the attacking team individually and together in one or another pitch zones depending on a situation, when they are situated initially and act according to provisions of zonal method of defense.

Zonal pressing suggests depriving the opponent of time and space for actions with the ball due to the ball location and opportunities of its delivery by players from the attacking team to one or another area of the pitch.

It is based on footballers' anthropometric, motive and technical capabilities to block one or another space in size across the width and length individually and in interaction with each other, situating differently.

There are basic elements of attacking and defensive play tactics in any team sport game with the ball, which include tactical actions performed by players individually and as a couple.

Football is not an exclusion in this context. Particularly there are several essential basic elements of zonal pressing tactics highlighted.

Their presence is explained by the following.

Zonal pressing may be realized in the context of various tactical schemes of play construction (with different correlation of players from different «play lines», players' position in «play lines» and number of «play lines»).

Regardless of schemes of play construction there are several types of typical local (with participation of one and two defending players) situations in defense.

Tactical individual actions and interactions of two defending players in these situations are effectively the same in different schemes of play construction, that suggests to consider these actions as basic elements of zonal pressing tactics.

This book provides a brief description of defensive actions in four typical local situation with participation of one and two defending players during the zonal pressing.

Special exercises for learning technique and raising the speed of actions performed during the zonal pressing, and acquisition of basic elements of zonal pressing tactics are suggested.

Tactical drills are recommended first of all for learning of young footballers 11-13 years old, so then it was easier for them to move to implement of zonal pressing tactics on the pitch of standard size in 11 on 11 play in the context of different schemes of play construction.

With that certain drills may be applied in professional teams also:

– if footballers do not have skills of defensive play using the zonal pressing;

– for correction of mistakes in individual actions or interactions of two defending players, repeating from game to game;

– with direct preparation for oncoming match with consideration for characteristics of attacking play construction by the opponent's team.

# LEGEND KEYS

Legend keys presented in figure 1 are used in describing players' actions and suggested drills in this book.

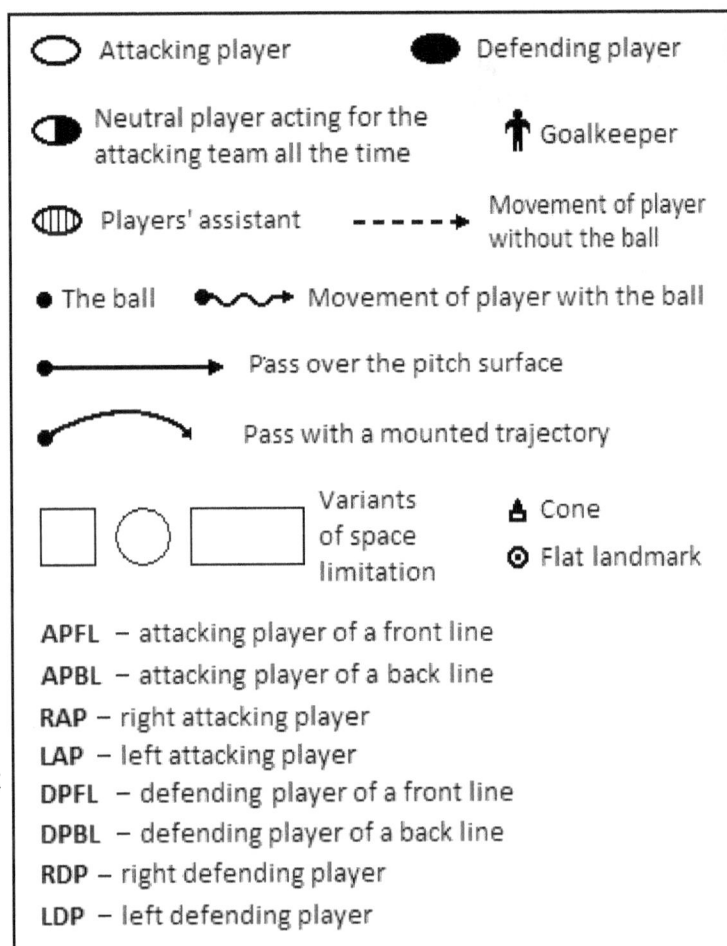

| | |
|---|---|
| ◯ Attacking player | ⬤ Defending player |
| ◑ Neutral player acting for the attacking team all the time | ⬆ Goalkeeper |
| ⬤ Players' assistant | ‑ ‑ ‑ ‑ ► Movement of player without the ball |
| ● The ball | ●〰► Movement of player with the ball |

●——————► Pass over the pitch surface

●⌒► Pass with a mounted trajectory

▢ ◯ ▭ Variants of space limitation    🔺 Cone    ◉ Flat landmark

**APFL** – attacking player of a front line
**APBL** – attacking player of a back line
**RAP** – right attacking player
**LAP** – left attacking player
**DPFL** – defending player of a front line
**DPBL** – defending player of a back line
**RDP** – right defending player
**LDP** – left defending player

Fig. 1. Legend keys used in describing players' actions and suggested drills

# For notes

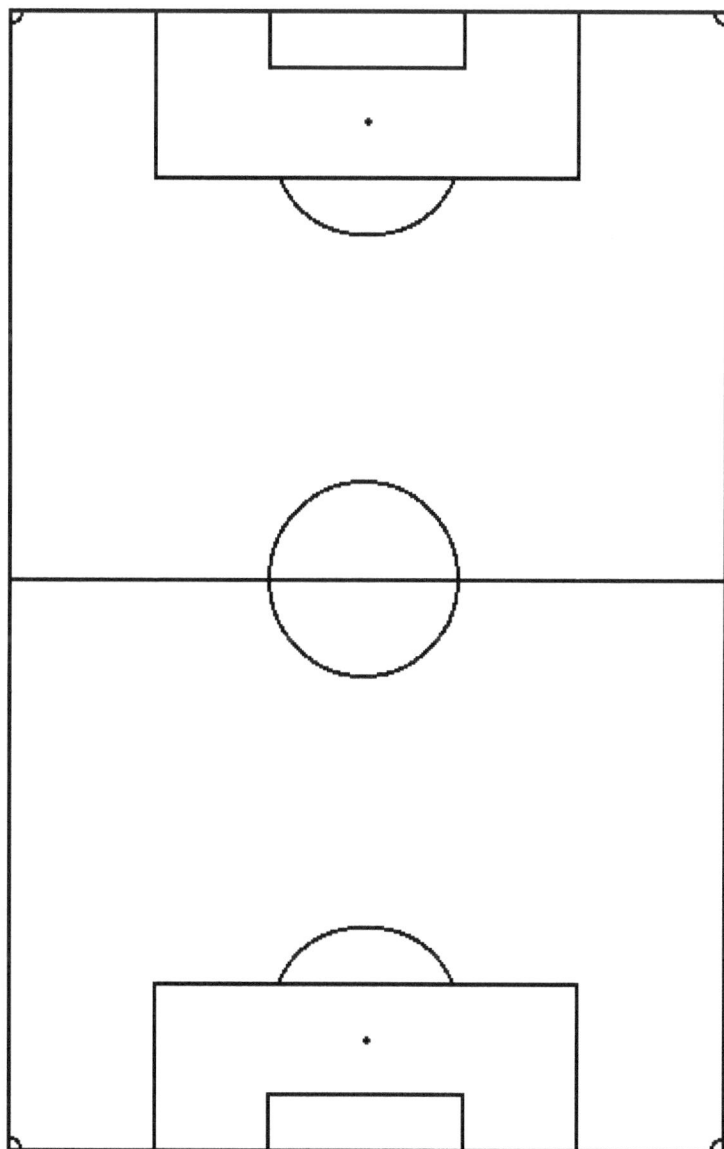

# CHAPTER 1.
# BRIEF DESCRIPTION OF
# BASIC ELEMENTS OF ZONAL
# PRESSING TACTICS

## 1. 1. Kinds of typical local situations of defensive play during the zonal pressing

In matches of teams applying zonal pressing, regardless of tactical schemes of play construction (correlation of players from different «play lines» and number of play lines), there are several types of typical local (with participation of one or two defending players) situations in defense (fig. 2).

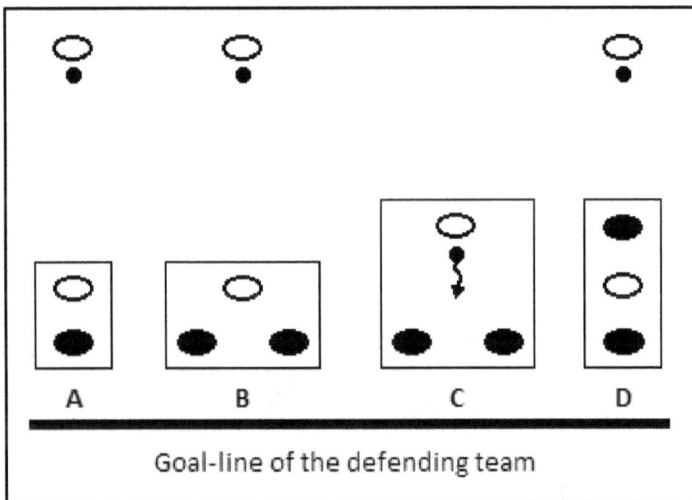

Goal-line of the defending team

Fig. 2. Kinds of typical situations of defensive play with participations of one and two defending players during the zonal pressing

First kind of situations – «one defending player on attacking player without the ball situated in front of him along the length of the pitch» (fig. 2A).

Second kind of situations – «two defending players on attacking player without the ball situated in front of them along the length of the pitch» (fig. 2B).

Third kind of situations – «two defending players on attacking player moving with the ball towards them along the length of the pitch» (fig. 2C).

Fourth kind of situations – «two defending players on attacking player without the ball situated between them along the length of the pitch» (fig. 2D).

Since actions of players from the defending team in each of listed above typical local situations are effectively the same in different tactical schemes of play construction, we can say that in these situations two defending players' actions and interactions are basic elements of zonal pressing tactics.

# 1. 2. Tactics in typical local situations of defensive play during the zonal pressing

## First basic element of zonal pressing tactics

Defending player's actions in «one on attacking player without the ball situated in front of him along the length of the pitch» situations suggest:

– controlling an opponent in «one's zone of responsibility»;

– restraint of the attacking player's attempts to come over the ball in space situated in front of defending player and behind him;

– pressing the attacking player out towards the half-way line, if play episode takes place on the defending team's half.

When performing these actions by the defending player it is essential to comply with the following provisions.

**First.** While controlling the attacking player without the ball in «zone of responsibility» defending player should be situated at some distance from the opponent between him and his own goal-line until the moment of sending the ball to the attacking player.

The «gap» between defending and attacking players varies depending on situation, but basically it should be such that on one hand the attacking player's partner possessing the ball believes that the ball can be sent at the attacking player's foot without risk, and on another the defending player makes it to play on the interception or tackle at the moment of opponent's reception of the ball.

**Second.** While performing a pass at the attacking player's foot defending player abruptly goes at the attacking player and tries to intercept the ball or attack the opponent at reception of the ball, anticipating the moment and the direction of sending of the ball and entering into physical contact with him.

**Third.** If the attacking player begins to move for reception of the ball into space behind the back of the defending player, while the attacking player's partner is ready to pass the ball on his way, the defending player should begin to move back to eliminate a possibility of attacking player receiving the ball.

**Fourth.** To press the attacking player without the ball out towards the half-way line, defending player should move around at some distance towards the half-way line and catch him offside. Therefore the attacking player will be forced to go back to space between his goal-line and the defending player.

Moving forward to the half-way line may be performed by the defending player at the moment when the ball cannot be sent by an opponent towards the goal-line of the defending team.

**Fifth.** The availability of a player from the attacking team possessing the ball to send the ball to a partner who begins to move into the space behind the defending player's back answers for a signal for the defending player to begin to move back (towards his goal-line) while pressing the attacking player out towards the half-way line.

## Second basic element
## of zonal pressing tactics

Defending players' actions in «two on attacking player without the ball situated between them along the length of the pitch» situations suggest:

– controlling the attacking player in «one's zone of responsibility»;

– restraint of his attempts to come over the ball in space in front of defending players (at foot) and behind them (on a way);

– pressing the attacking player out towards the half-way line, if play episode takes place on the defending team's half.

In these situations defending players' interaction comes down to:

– «transfer» of the attacking player under partner's control in cases of this player switching from one defending player's «zone of responsibility» to another;

– choice of actions priority while restraint of attacking player's attempts to receive the ball at his foot;

– covering each other at attempts to intercept the ball sent to the attacking player.

While performing these actions it is necessary for defending players to comply with the following provisions.

**First.** While controlling the attacking player in own «zone of responsibility» before the moment of sending the ball to him it is necessary for defending players to locate at 7-8 meters approx parallel to each other along the length of the pitch and at some distance from the opponent between him and own goal-line.

The gap between the attacking player and defending players may vary depending on situation, but basically should be such that in case of sending the ball at the attacking player's foot one of defending players can play on the interception or tackle at the moment of opponent's reception of the ball.

**Second.** While performing a pass at the attacking player's foot one of attacking players, anticipating the moment and the direction of a  pass, should abruptly go  at the attacking player to intercept the ball or attack the opponent at reception of the ball, while another should drift towards the point, where the partner was situated before the moment of going at the attacking player. It should be the defending player, in whose «zone of responsibility» the attacking player tries to come over the ball, who goes at the attacking player.

**Third.** If the attacking player begins to move for reception of the ball into space behind the back of the defending player, while the attacking player's partner is ready to pass the ball on his way, both defending players should begin to move back to eliminate a possibility of attacking player receiving the ball.

**Fourth.** To press the attacking player without the ball out towards the half-way line, defending players should move around at some distance towards the half-way line and catch him offside, from whence the last will be forced to go back to space between defending players and the goal-line of the attacking team.

Moving forward may be performed by defending players at the moment when the ball cannot be sent by an opponent towards the goal-line of the defending team.

**Fifth.** The availability of a player from the attacking team possessing the ball to send the ball to a partner who begins to move into the space behind the defending player's back answers for a signal for defending players to begin to move back while pressing the attacking player out towards the half-way line.

### Third basic element
### of zonal pressing tactics

Defending players' actions in «two on attacking player moving with the ball towards them along the length of the pitch» situations suggest the following.

**First.** The defending player, in whose «zone of responsibility» the attacking player with the ball moves, faces the opponent first.

Getting ready to tacking or knocking the ball out and beginning to perform these actions, this defending player should eliminate a possibility of attacking player going with the ball towards through space, located on the side opposite to where the second defending player is situated, and provoke the attacking player to move towards the second defending player.

**Second.** While the defending player, who faces the attacking player first, gets ready to accomplish a tackle or knocking the ball out, the second one begins to move towards partner.

He moves so that to be 3-4 meters across the width and 1-2 meters along the length of the pitch closer than the defending player to own goal-line, i.e. diagonally to the partner relative to the goal-line, by the moment when the attacking player begins the performance of outplaying the defending player who closes with him first.

**Third.** If the defending player, who faces the attacking player first, is not able to tackle or knock the ball out from him, this has to be done by the second defending player, because:

– the attacking player «stumbles» upon him while trying to go with the ball forward through the space between two defending players;

– the has a possibility to cover the partner, when the attacking player succeeds in outplaying the defending player who faces him first, from the side opposite to where the second defending player is situated.

## Fourth basic element
## of zonal pressing tactics

Defending players' actions in «two on attacking player without the ball situated between them along the length of the pitch» situations suggest the following.

**First.** While controlling the attacking player without the ball it is necessary for defending players to be situated at relatively short distance from each other for observing necessary compact arrangement along the length of the pitch (from 8-10 meters to 13-15 meters depending on situation).

**Second.** While the ball is sent at the attacking player's foot, defending players should vice the opponent through following actions:

– the defending players of a back line abruptly goes at the attacking player and tries to intercept the ball or attack the opponent at reception of the ball, anticipating the moment and the direction of sending of the ball and entering into physical contact with him;

– after the ball has crossed the line of his position, the defending player of a front line turn his face towards his goal-line and quickly move directly at the attacking player.

**Third.** If the attacking player begins to open into space behind the back of the defending player of a back line, this player moves towards his goal-line, having timely responded to the beginning of the attacking player's movement, and tries to keep the gap between the opponent and himself of 3-4 meters before the moment of sending the ball to the opponent.

**Fourth.** While sending the ball on the attacking player's way into space behind the back of the defending player of a front line, the defending player of a front line should move towards his goal-line after the ball crosses the line of his position to keep a compact arrangement of defending players' position along the length of the pitch, if he fails to intercept the ball.

# 1. 3. Kinds of movements performed by defending players during the zonal pressing

When implementing the zonal pressing, defending players use different kinds of movements depending on problems they have to solve in the course of play situations.

Main problems for the defending player during the zonal pressing in typical local situations of defensive play are:

– controlling an opponent in «one's zone of responsibility»;

– restraint of the attacking player's attempts to come over the ball in space situated in front of defending players and behind them;

– pressing the opponent out towards the half-way line, if play episode takes place on the defending team's half;

– covering partner while he is trying to intercept or tackle the ball.

Observing matches of teams of high qualification has shown that defending players use the following kinds of movements for solving these problems:

– while controlling the opponent in «own zone of responsibility» – local movements to the left or right, back and forth;

– while the attacking player is trying to possess the ball (sent at the foot) in space in front of defending players – movements frontward;

– while the attacking player is trying to possess the ball in space behind them (sent on a way) – movements backwards and sideways with the subsequent transition both to movement in the same direction frontwise and movement in the opposite direction (frontwise) or to the side;

– while pressing the attacking player out towards the halfway line – movements frontwise with the subsequent transition to movement in the opposite direction backwards or sideways;

– while covering each other – movements sideways, frontwise and backwards.

## 1. 4. Resume

The efficiency of defensive play in applying zonal pressing is due to defending players' opportunities, on one hand, to be on the ball first in case of a pass into space behind their back, and on the other to attack the opponent situated in front of them along the length of the pitch if the ball is sent at his foot.

The degree of these opportunities realization depends on two major factors:

– footballers' ability to anticipate development of play situations, i.e. act with space-time advance of events at the pitch;

– players' abilities to act as quick as possible while trying to intercept and tackle the ball, which requires speed of movements in different ways.

By virtue of brief description of basic elements of zonal pressing tactics the following can be concluded.

Actions of players from the defending team in typical local situations during the zonal pressing are specific and completely differ from their actions in similar situations during man-to-man marking.

In this regard it is important for footballers to acquire basic elements of zonal pressing to be able to act successfully when implementing this tactics in the context of different tactical schemes of play. In this case:

a) it would be easier for young footballers to move to implementation of zonal pressing in 11 on 11 games on the pitch of standard size at the appropriate age;

b) professional footballers would be able to adapt while transition to using zonal pressing in the context of another tactical scheme of team play construction quicker.

# For notes

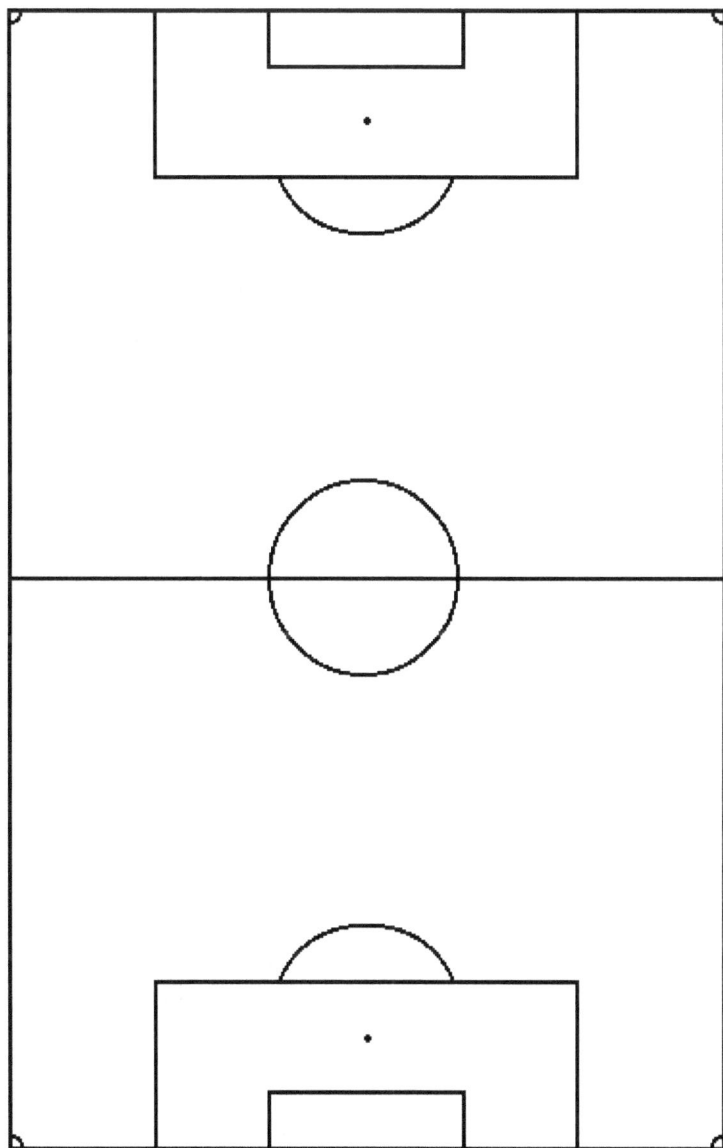

# CHAPTER 2.
# CHARACTERISTICS
# OF LEARNING THE BASIC
# ELEMENTS OF ZONAL
# PRESSING TACTICS

Learning the basic elements of zonal pressing tactics suggests three main sections of work:
– learning the technique and raising the speed of movement performed by defending players during the zonal pressing;
– study the specificity of actions in typical local situation with participation of one and two defending players during the zonal pressing;
– using acquired basic elements of zonal pressing tactics in games.

There may be marked several characteristics in training method of basic elements of zonal pressing.

**First.** Drills of standard and game character, suggested for learning tactical skills of play using the zonal pressing, are performed in small areas of the pitch and with the participation of several players. This stipulates that these drills are fully understandable for junior footballers, at least from 10-11 y.o., as shown by experience.

**Second.** With that young footballers may not yet show the level of precision in passing with the leg, which is necessary for qualitative performance of tactical drills and subsequently for learning basic elements of zonal pressing tactics, on all occasions. Therefore there may be provided passes by hand not only by goalkeepers, but also by in-field players, in certain drills.

**Third.** For quicker consolidation of proper tactical skills of defensive actions by players it is important that attacking players act rigorously in a certain way and with a strictly defined activity at least at first. In this regard in some drills attacking players' actions are regulated in such a way that they act only as defending players' assistants.

**Fourth.** Another characteristic of learning the basic elements of zonal pressing tactics is that initially the observance of offside may represent interference to learning necessary tactical skills by young footballers. In this regard definite part of drills both of standard and game character should take place with non-observance of offside approximately up to 13 years old.

**Fifth.** While learning tactics during the zonal pressing in typical local situations with participation of one and two defending players two balls may be used in certain drills. By using the second ball that may be sent both with leg and hand, there may be simulated different variants of play situations development and pointed out directions of players' movement to one or another area of the pitch.

**Sixth.** Young footballers may begin to learn the technique of movements specific for zonal pressing virtually from the beginning of playing football (from 7-8 years old) in the context of familiarization with various motive skills.

**Seventh.** Further on as players grow older, it is necessary to demand the maximum movement speed of them while performing such movements. The most favorable for raising the speed of movements at short distance in children and youth age is 11-14 years old.

# CHAPTER 3.
# LEARNING THE TECHNIQUE
# AND RAISING THE SPEED
# OF MOVEMENTS PERFORMED
# DURING THE ZONAL PRESSING

## 3. 1. Tasks and emphasis of the work

While learning the technique and raising the speed of movements performed during the zonal pressing, it is necessary to learn footballers quickly:
– move frontwise and backwards;
– change the direction of movement to the opposite and to side;
– switch from moving backwards to moving in the same direction frontwise.

In addressing these problems the attention is focused on several points.

**First.** Concerning the technique of movements it should be noted that for a quick change of direction and way of movement it is important for players not to be stiff-legged, hands hold not completely down, but bent at elbows, and to perform dynamic movements back and forth with them.

**Second.** During the zonal pressing players are required not only to start moving quickly, but also to stop so. In this regard it is important to pay particular attention to raising the speed of deceleration performance by them while moving with a high speed.

**Third.** Exercises suggesting footballers' rivalry are the most effective for raising the speed of movement. It could be drills suggesting direct countering of players to one another or their contest to see how performs set actions faster and more precisely.

# 3. 2. Drills for learning the technique and raising the speed of movements performed during the zonal pressing

### Task 1. Moving frontwise at first, and then in the opposite direction backwards

| Task description | Requirements for task performance quality |
|---|---|
| Players are situated at the marked line face to balls set a few meters away.<br>On signal players move frontwise to «their» ball quickly and touch it with a foot, then move back backwards and try to cross the marked line first.<br><br><br><br>Distance between balls and players varies from 4-5 to 8-10 meters.<br>**Variant:** moving frontwise to the ball – backwards to the marked line – face to the ball<br><br> | – players should perform running forward and back at a maximum speed trying to beat partner;<br>– players should change the direction of movement to the opposite as quick as possible;<br>– players should keep arms bent at elbows and perform movements back and forth with them dynamically, moving backwards;<br>– players should occasionally glance at the point they are moving to, moving backwards |

## Task 2 Moving backwards at first, and then in the opposite direction frontwise

| Task description | Requirements for task performance quality |
|---|---|
| Players are situated at balls set few meters away from the marked line back to this line.<br>On signal players move backwards to the marked line quickly and cross it, then move back frontwise and try to touch «their» ball with a foot first.<br><br><br><br>Distance between balls and the marked line varies from 4-5 to 8-10 meters.<br>**Variant:** moving backwards to the marked line – face to the ball – backwards to the marked line<br><br> | – players should perform running forward and back at a maximum speed trying to beat partner;<br>– players should change the direction of movement to the opposite as quick as possible;<br>– players should keep arms bent at elbows and perform movements back and forth with them dynamically, moving backwards;<br>– players should occasionally glance at the point they are moving to, moving backwards |

## Task 3. Moving frontwise or backwards at first, then to the side

| Task description | Requirements for task performance quality |
|---|---|
| Players are situated at the marked line face to flat landmarks set a few meters away. Balls are set in parallel to the marked line few meters to the side from landmarks. <br> On signal players move quickly face to «their» landmark at first, then to the side and try to touch «their» ball with a foot first. | – players should perform running forward and back and to the side at a maximum speed trying to beat partner; <br> – players should change the direction of movement to the side as quick as possible; <br> – players should keep arms bent at elbows and perform movements back and forth with them dynamically, moving backwards; <br> – players should occasionally glance at the point they are moving to, moving backwards |
| Distance between landmarks and the marked line varies from 4-5 to 8-10 meters. Balls are set to the left and to the right of landmarks at 3-5 meters. <br> **Variant:** moving backwards to the landmark – to the side to the ball | |

25

## Task 4. Moving along a zigzag trajectory frontwise and backwards

| Task description | Requirements for task performance quality |
|---|---|
| Two lines are marked in parallel to each other at 15 meters. Four flat landmarks are set zigzag few (3-6) meters away from one another. Players are situated at one of marked lines in a position to the opposite line:<br>a) face;<br>b) back.<br>On signal player move quickly from landmark to landmark and try to cross the opposite marked line first, moving in a position:<br>a) fronwise;<br>b) backwards.<br><br><br><br>**Variant:** points of benchmarking are varied by distance relative to each other and defined direction of players' movement | – players should perform running backwards and frontwise at a maximum speed trying to beat partner;<br>– players should change the direction of movement to the side as quick as possible;<br>– players should keep arms bent at elbows and perform movements back and forth with them dynamically, moving backwards;<br>– players should occasionally glance at the point they are moving to, moving backwards |

## Task 5. Moving backwards at first, then U-turn and moving in the same direction frontwise

| Task description | Requirements for task performance quality |
|---|---|
| 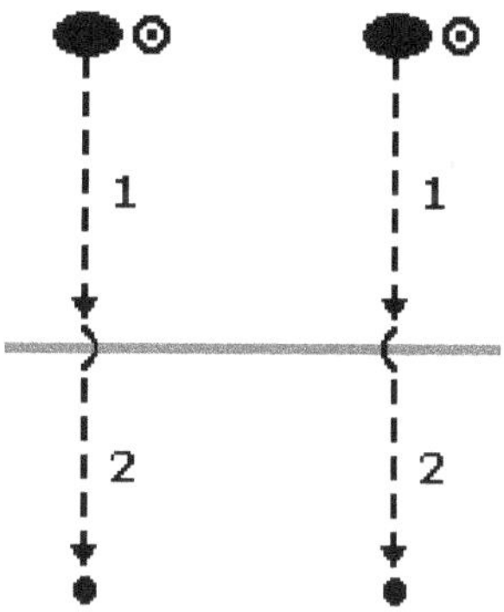 Players are situated at flat landmarks set few meters away from balls back to balls.<br>Parallel boundary line is marked between nominal lines on which landmarks and balls are set.<br>On signal players quickly move backwards to the marked line, make U-turn and then move frontwise to «their» ball and try to touch it first with the foot (fig. 1). | – players should perform running backwards and frontwise at a maximum speed trying to beat partner;<br>– players should keep arms bent at elbows and perform movements back and forth with them dynamically, moving backwards;<br>– players should occasionally glance at the point they are moving to, moving backwards;<br>– players should perform turn to move frontwise at a maximum speed, lowering the speed of movement to a lesser extent with that |

**Fig. 1**

| | |
|---|---|
| Distance between landmarks and the marked line varies from 4-5 to 8-10 meters. Balls are set at 4-8 meters from the marked line. | |

Task 5 continuation

**Variants:**
a) U-turn is performed through the right and left side;
b) balls are set so that players perform a turn to a slightly lower value than 180 degrees, and after a turn move to «their» balls diagonally relative to direction of movement before the turn (fig. 2 and 3)

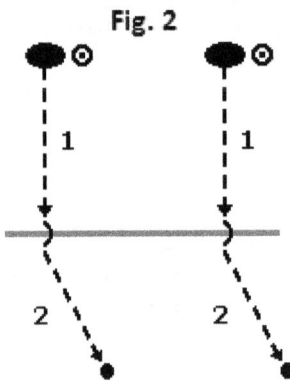

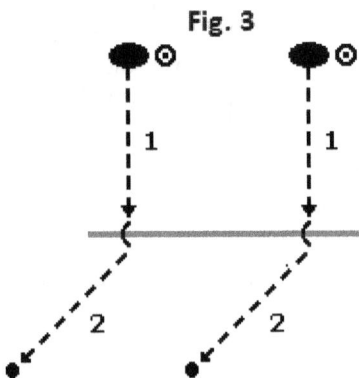

**Fig. 2**

**Fig. 3**

**Task 6. Moving backwards at first, then U-turn and moving the same direction frontwise with a view to beat the attacking player moving to the ball frontwise all the time**

| Task description | Requirements for task performance quality |
|---|---|
| A «corridor» 15 meters long and 3 meters wide is marked. Ball is set on one of lines bordering the «corridor» across the width. A line bordering a zone 3 by 3 meters in the «corridor» is marked 3 meters away from this line. One attacking and one defending player are situated: <br> – attacking player – on the «corridor» line opposite relative to the ball, face to ball; <br> – defending player – in «corridor» 3 meters away from the attacking player, back to ball (fig. 1). <br><br> <br> Fig. 1   3m   15m   3m   3m | – players should perform running to the ball at a maximum speed, trying to touch it first; <br> – defending player should necessarily move backwards up to the zone 3 by 3 meters; <br> – defending player should keep arms bent at elbows and perform movements back and forth with them dynamically, moving backwards; <br> – defending player should occasionally glance towards the ball, moving backward; <br> – defending player should perform a U-turn at a maximum speed; <br> – defending player should the ball while falling if necessary to perform first touch of the ball |

Task 6 continuation

On signal players quickly move to the ball and try to touch it with a foot first. Defending player moves to the ball backwards at first (fig. 2), then makes a U-turn in zone 3 by 3 meters and moves frontwise (fig. 3)

**Fig. 2**

Corridor zone in which the defending player should move backwards

**Fig. 3**

Corridor zone in which the defending player should move frontwise

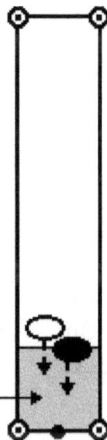

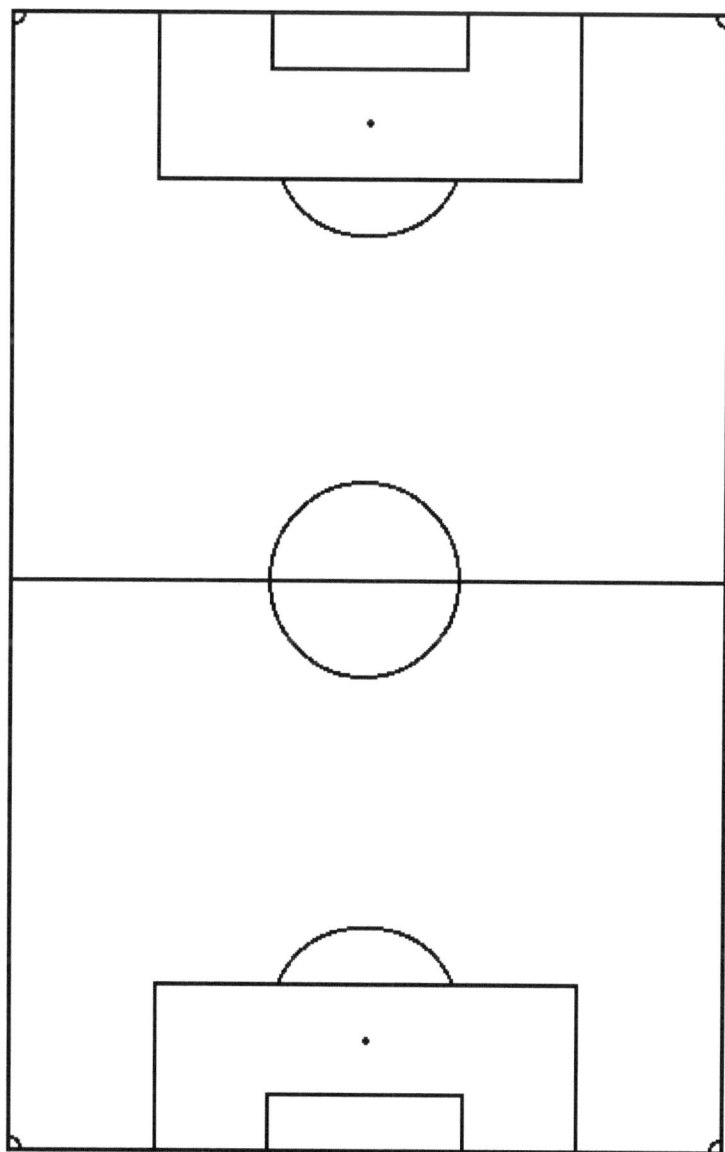

# For notes

# CHAPTER 4.
# DEFENDING PLAYERS' LEARNING OF ACTIONS IN «ONE ON ATTACKING PLAYER WITHOUT THE BALL SITUATED IN FRONT OF HIM ALONG THE LENGTH OF THE PITCH» SITUATIONS

## 4. 1. Tasks and emphasis of the work

While learning the defensive play in «one on the attacking player without the ball situated in front of him along the length of the pitch» it is necessary to learn footballers three main kinds of action.

**First.** To control the opponent not possessing the ball in «own zone of responsibility».

**Second.** To prevent attacking player's attempts to possess the ball after a pass at his foot or on his way.

**Third.** To press the attacking player out towards the halfway line.

In the course of learning these actions the attention is focused on development of players' abilities and skills of psychomotor character as follows:

– eye control of a marked opponent and the attacking player possessing the ball;

– anticipation of a moment and direction of sending the ball to a marked player basing on actions of his partner performing a pass;

– speed of movements to the ball sent at the opponent's foot or on his way.

With that variation of distance and direction of passes to the attacking player is effective methodological technique.

# 4. 2. Drills for learning actions while controlling the attacking players in «one's zone of responsibility»

**Task 1. Controlling the attacking player without the ball during his local movements to the left and to the right**

| Task description | Requirements for task performance quality |
|---|---|
| 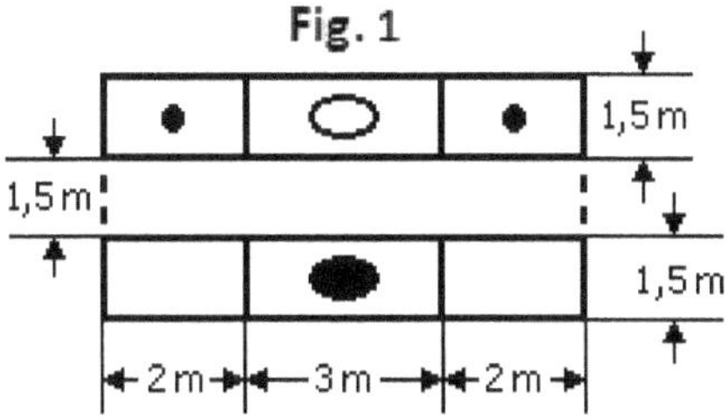 Two corridors 7 meters long and 1,5 meters wide are marked in parallel to each other at 1,5 meters. Each corridor is divided into three zones: two lateral 2 meters long each and the middle 3 meters long. <br> One attacking player and one defending player are situated in middle zones of different corridors face to each other. <br> Balls are set in the middle of lateral zones of a corridor where the attacking player is situated (fig. 1). | – players should change the direction of movement to the opposite as quick as possible; <br> – the attacking player should touch the ball having performed at least four and no more than eight body movements in different directions; <br> – the attacking player should touch the ball while necessarily being at that moment both legs in the corridor zone where the ball is set; <br> – while performing movements the attacking player should not turn his back to the defending player; |

**Fig. 1**

| | |
|---|---|
| On signal the attacking player begins to move through his corridor to the left and to the right, changing the direction of movement and using dummies. | |

Task 1 continuation

| | |
|---|---|
| While moving to the left and to the right in his corridor, the defending player should try to be symmetric about the attacking player. After 4-8 changes in direction of movement to the left and to the right the attacking player should one of balls with both hands, providing that he is both legs in the zone of a corridor where the ball is set. If the defending player is both legs in his corridor zone, that is symmetric to the zone where the attacking player touches the ball, in the moment when the attacking player touches the ball, the former wins in this repetition of the task (fig. 2). Otherwise, the attacking player wins (fig. 3). | – while moving, the defending player should not be stiff-legged, but slightly bent in the knees; – while moving, the defending player should work with legs quickly |

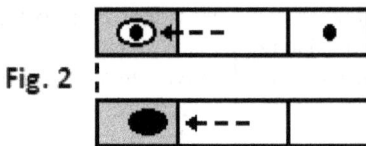

Fig. 2

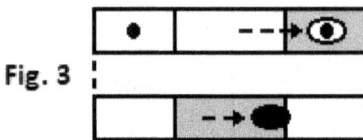

Fig. 3

The duration of one task repetition is no longer than 5-6 seconds.
Number of repeats – 8-10 times with the rest pause 5-10 seconds depending on the duration of previous repeat

## Task 2. Controlling the attacking player without the ball during his local movements back and forth

| Task description | Requirements for task performance quality |
|---|---|
| Two zones 3 on 3 meters is marked at 1 meter, divided into three parallel to each other zones 1 meter wide.<br>One attacking player and one defending player are situated in the middle of different zones face to each other.<br>On near and distant relative to the opposite zone lines, that border the zone where the attacking player is situated, balls are set: one ball slightly to the right, and another slightly to the left relative to the attacking player (fig. 1). | – players should change the direction of movement to the opposite as quick as possible;<br>– the attacking player should touch the ball having performed at least four and no more than eight body movements in different directions;<br>– the attacking player should touch the ball while necessarily being at that moment both legs in the corridor where the ball is set;<br>– while performing movements the attacking player should not turn his back to the defending player;<br>– while moving, the defending player should not be stiff-legged, but slightly bent in the knees; |
|
Fig. 1 | – while moving, the defending player should work with legs quickly |
| On signal the attacking player begins to move in his zone back and forth, changing the direction of movement and using dummies. | |

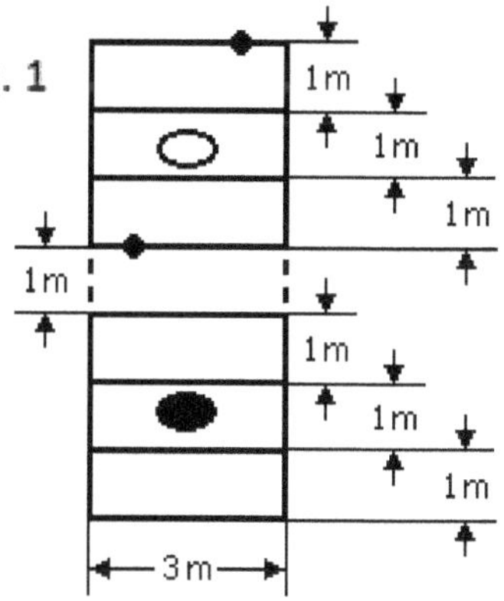

35

Task 2 continuation

Moving back and forth in his zone, the defending player tries to be approx. 3 meters away from the attacking player.

After 4-8 changes in direction of movement back and forth the attacking player should one of balls with both hands, providing that he is both legs in the corridor where the ball is set.

If the defending player is both legs in the corridor which is marked 3 meters away from the corridor where the attacking player touches the ball, in the moment when the attacking player touches the ball, the former wins in this repetition of the task (fig. 2). Otherwise, the attacking player wins (fig. 3).

**Fig. 2**     **Fig. 3**

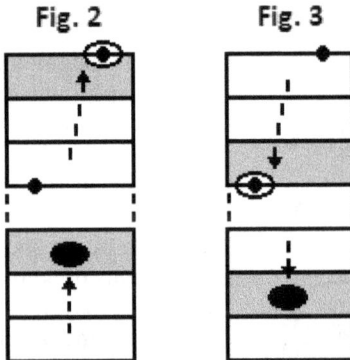

The duration of one task repetition is no longer than 5-6 seconds.

Number of repeats – 8-10 times with the rest pause 5-10 seconds depending on the duration of previous repeat

## 4. 3. Drills for learning actions while passing the ball at the attacking player's foot

**Task 1. Controlling the attacking player without the ball during his local movements to the left and to the right and interception of the ball sent at his foot**

| Task description | Requirements for task performance quality |
|---|---|
| The corridor 10 meters long and 1 meter wide is marked. Boundary line 10 meters long is marked in parallel ti the corridor 3 meters away from it.<br>Two attacking and one defending players are situated:<br>– the attacking player with the ball – 10 meters from the corridor on the opposite to boundary line side face to it;<br>– the attacking player without the ball – in corridor face to partner;<br>– the defending player – near boundary line face to attacking players (fig. 1). 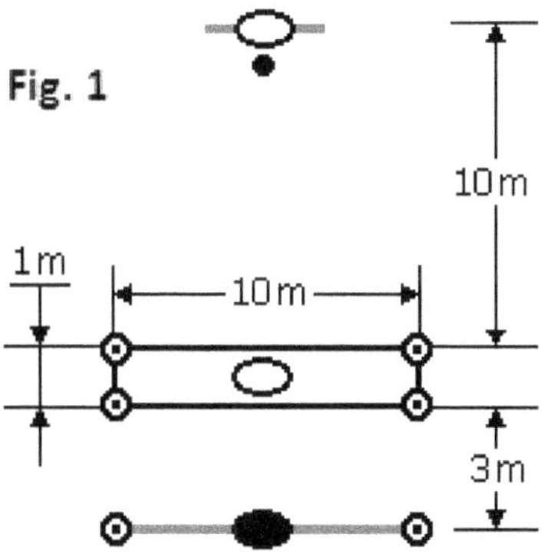 | – while controlling actions of the attacking player without the ball, the defending player should be near boundary line up to the moment of sending the ball to this player and see actions of the attacking player possessing the ball with that;<br>– while controlling actions of the attacking player without the ball, the defending player should not be stiff-legged, but slightly bent in the knees, and be ready to go for interception of the ball in any moment; |

Fig. 1
10 m
1 m
10 m
3 m

## Task 1 continuation

On signal the attacking player without the ball begins to move medium tempo through the corridor to the left and to the right and gets ready to receive the ball at the foot.

The defending player moves along boundary line to the left and to the right, controlling actions of the attacking player without the ball and keeping an eye on the attacking player possessing the ball.

After 3-5 changes of movement direction along the corridor by the attacking player the attacking player possessing the ball sends it at the partner's foot over the pitch surface with a lower speed.

The attacking player in the corridor tries to possess the ball staying within the corridor.

At the moment of a pass performance the defending player abruptly goes forward (fig. 2), intercepts the ball and moves with it forward at 5-7 meters (fig. 3).

– while controlling actions of the attacking player without the ball, the defending player should take the most comfortable position during interception of the ball;

– the defending player should anticipate the moment and the direction of a pass by the attacking player on his preparative actions to a pass performance and beginning of strike motion;

– the defending player should go forward for interception of the ball at a maximum speed;

– the attacking player in corridor should try to possess the ball within the corridor and not to act with a maximum activity

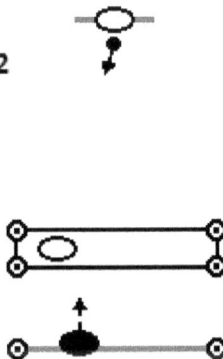

**Fig. 2**

Task 1 continuation

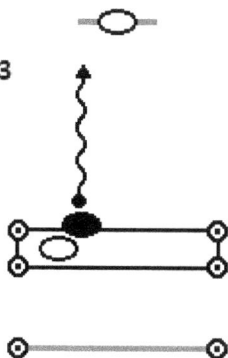

Fig. 3

**Variants:**
a) the attacking player with the ball is situated at different distance from the corridor and sends balls to a partner with a different speed;
b) the attacking player with the ball is situated and sends balls to a partner at different angles relative to the corridor;
c) the attacking player with the ball simulates performance of a pass to the partner one or two times at first, and then sends the ball to him. Responding to the dummy strike motion, the defending player steps forward, beginning outing for interception of the ball, but seeing that a pass to the attacking player doesn't follow, steps back, restoring the distance between himself and the marked opponent approx. 3 meters.
At the real pass to the attacking player the defending player abruptly goes forward, intercepts the ball and moves with it forward at 5-7 meters

**Task 2. Controlling the attacking player without the ball while he is moving back along with creation of 3 meters distance from the opponent until the moment of a pass and interception of the ball sent at the attacking player's foot**

| Task description | Requirements for task performance quality |
|---|---|
| Four parallel lines 5 meters long are marked at a distance:<br>– second line at 10 meters from the first;<br>– third line at 3 meters from the second;<br>– fourth line at 7 meters from the third.<br>Two attacking and one defending players are situated:<br>– the attacking player with the ball – at the first line face to the second line;<br>– the attacking player without the ball and the defending player – at the fourth line face to the attacking player with the ball (fig. 1).<br><br><br>**Fig. 1**<br>1st line<br>2nd line<br>3rd line<br>4th line<br>10 m<br>3 m<br>7 m | – while controlling actions of the attacking player without the ball, the defending player should be approx. 3 meters away from him up to the moment of sending the ball to this player and see actions of the attacking player possessing the ball with that;<br>– while controlling actions of the attacking player without the ball, the defending player should not be stiff-legged, but slightly bent in the knees;<br>– while controlling actions of the attacking player without the ball, the defending player should take the most comfortable position during interception of the ball; |

Task 2 continuation

On signal the attacking player without the ball begins to move medium tempo to the second line, stops at it and gets ready to receive the ball at the foot.

The defending player moves after the attacking player so that to be at the third line to the moment, when the last reaches the second (fig. 2).

**Fig. 2**

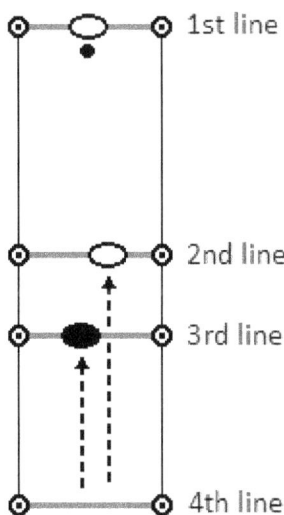

- the attacking player possessing the ball should perform a pass at the partner's foot after he gets into position at the second boundary line;
- the defending player should anticipate the moment and the direction of a pass by the attacking player on his preparative actions to a pass performance and beginning of strike motion;
- the defending player should go forward for interception of the ball at a maximum speed;
- the attacking player without the ball should try to possess the ball in area near the second boundary line and not to act with a maximum activity

When the attacking player without the ball gets to the second line, partner sends the ball at his foot over the pitch surface with a **lower** speed.

At the moment of a pass performance the defending player abruptly goes forward (fig. 3), intercepts the ball and moves with it forward at 5-7 meters (fig. 4)

Task 2 continuation

**Fig. 3**

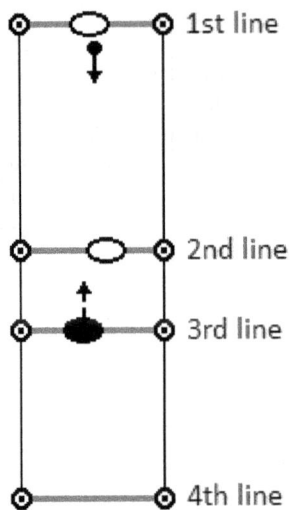

1st line

2nd line

3rd line

4th line

**Fig. 4**

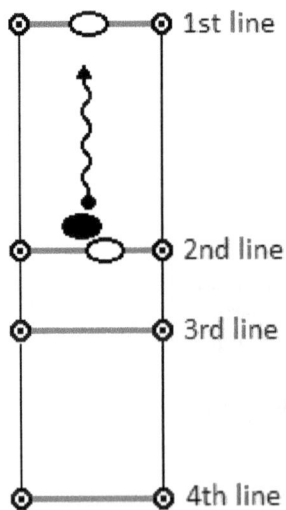

1st line

2nd line

3rd line

4th line

### Task 3. Controlling the attacking player without the ball during his local movements to the left and to the right, coming into contact with him when he comes over the ball and restoring the 3 meters distance from the opponent after performing a pass

| Task description | Requirements for task performance quality |
|---|---|
| The corridor 10 meters long and 1 meter wide is marked. Boundary line 10 meters long is marked in parallel ti the corridor 3 meters away from it.<br>Two attacking and one defending players are situated:<br>– the attacking player with the ball – 10 meters from the corridor on the opposite to boundary line side face to it;<br>– the attacking player without the ball – in corridor face to partner;<br>– the defending player – near boundary line face to attacking players (fig. 1).<br><br><br>**Fig. 1**<br><br>On signal the attacking player without the ball begins to move medium tempo through the corridor to the left and to the right and gets ready to receive the ball at the foot. | – while controlling actions of the attacking player without the ball, the defending player should be near boundary line up to the moment of sending the ball to this player and see actions of the attacking player possessing the ball with that;<br>– while controlling actions of the attacking player without the ball, the defending player should not be stiff-legged, but slightly bent in the knees, and be ready to go for interception of the ball in any moment;<br>– the defending player should come into contact with the opponent, without breaking football rules; |

43

## Task 3 continuation

The defending player moves along boundary line to the left and to the right, controlling actions of the attacking player without the ball and keeping an eye on the attacking player possessing the ball.

After 3-5 changes of movement direction along the corridor by the attacking player the attacking player possessing the ball sends it at the partner's foot over the pitch surface with a **high** speed.

The attacking player in the corridor tries to possess the ball staying within the corridor.

At the moment of a pass performance the defending player abruptly goes forward for interception of the ball. Failing to intercept the ball which the attacking player come over face to partner, the defending player enters into physical contact with the opponent, but doesn't prevent him from returning the ball to the partner with a second or a third touch (fig. 2).

– after the attacking player he pressed performs a pass to the partner, the defending player should quickly move back to boundary line;

– while moving backwards, the defending player should see actions of the attacking player without the ball and the attacking player possessing the ball;

– defending player should keep arms bent at elbows and perform movements back and forth with them dynamically, moving backwards

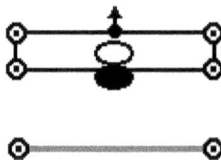

**Fig. 2**

Task 3 continuation

In conditions of physical contact with the defending player the attacking player returns the ball to his partner with a second or a third touch.

After the attacking player performs a pass to the partner, the defending player quickly moves to boundary line, moving backwards (fig. 3).

**Fig. 3**

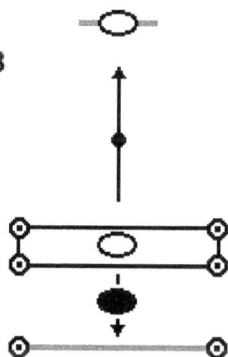

**Variants:**

a) the attacking player with the ball is situated and sends balls to a partner at different angles relative to the corridor;

b) directly after the defending player, having broken contact with the opponent, gets back to boundary line, the attacking player possessing the ball sends it to his partner for a second time.

The defending player abruptly goes forward, intercepts the ball and moves with it forward at 5-7 meters

# 4. 4. Drills for learning actions while passing the ball on the attacking player's way

## Task 1. Beating the attacking player trying to come over one of two balls in area behind the defending player's back

| Task description | Requirements for task performance quality |
|---|---|
| Four parallel lines 8 meters long are marked at a distance:<br>– second line at 3 meters from the first;<br>– third line at 5 meters from the second;<br>– fourth line at 7 meters from the third.<br>One ball is set at each end of the fourth line.<br>One attacking and one defending player are situated:<br>– the attacking player – at the first line face to the second line;<br>– the defending player – at the second line opposite to the attacking player face to him (fig. 1).<br>Suddenly the attacking player begins to move quickly to the third line.<br>The defending player moves back backwards and tries to keep the distance from the opponent approx. 3 meters (fig. 2).<br>Having reached the third line the attacking player begins to move quickly to one of two balls, trying to touch it first with a foot.<br>The defending player turns and moves frontwise to the ball, which the attacking player has begun to move to, trying to touch that ball with a foot earlier than the opponent (fig. 3). | – the attacking player should move at a maximum speed to the area behind the defending player's back;<br>– the defending player should move backwards at a maximum speed and try to keep the distance from the opponent approx. 3 meters;<br>– having begun moving to one of balls after crossing the third boundary line, the attacking player should not change the direction of movement any more;<br>– the defending player should timely identify, which ball the attacking player has decided to come over; |

## Task 1 continuation

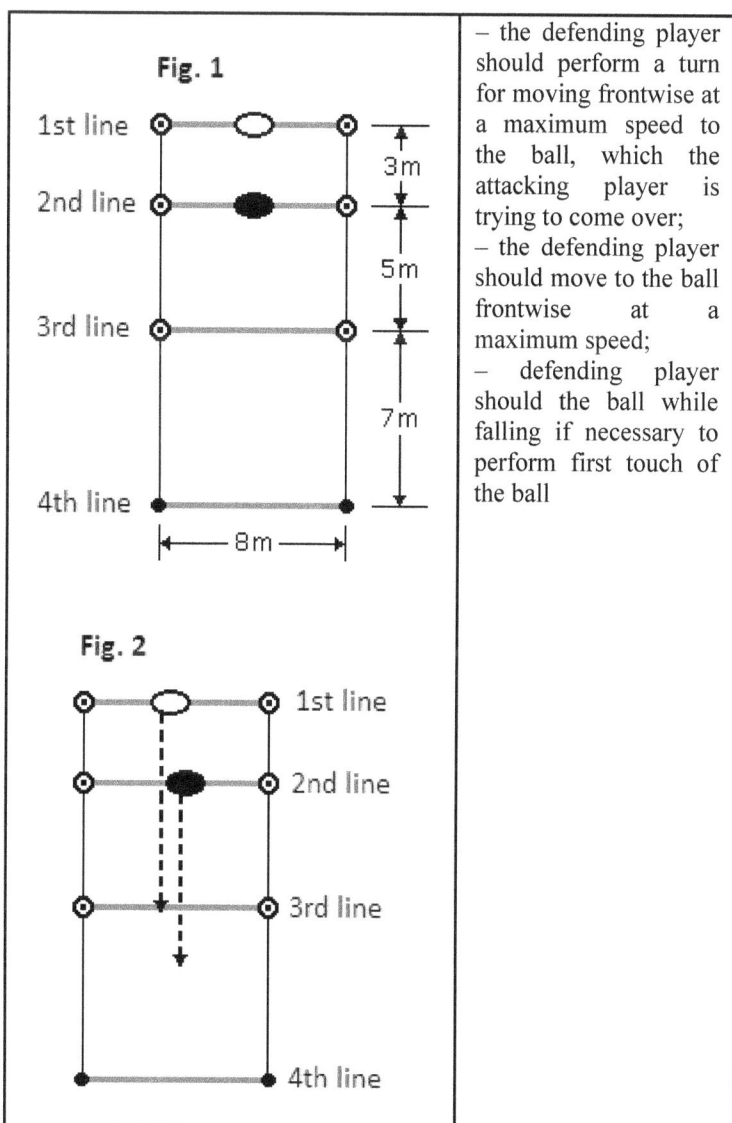

**Fig. 1**

1st line

2nd line

3m

5m

3rd line

7m

4th line

8m

**Fig. 2**

1st line

2nd line

3rd line

4th line

– the defending player should perform a turn for moving frontwise at a maximum speed to the ball, which the attacking player is trying to come over;

– the defending player should move to the ball frontwise at a maximum speed;

– defending player should the ball while falling if necessary to perform first touch of the ball

Task 1 continuation

**Fig. 3**

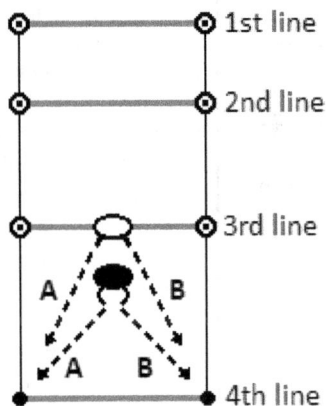

**Variants:**
a) directions of the attacking player's movement to the third line are varied;
b) points of the attacking player's initial position at the first line (fig. 4)

**Fig. 4**

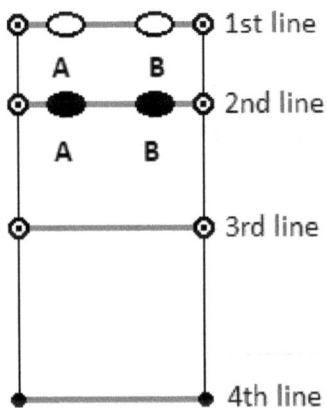

## Task 2. Coming over the ball sent on the attacking player's way into the area behind the defending player's back

| Task description | Requirements for task performance quality |
|---|---|
| Playground 15 meters long and 10 meters wide is marked, divided into 2 zones 3 and 12 meters long.<br>Boundary line 10 meters long is marked opposite to the short side of the playground 5 meters from it.<br>Two attacking and one defending players are situated:<br>– the attacking player with the ball – at boundary line;<br>– the attacking player without the ball – at the short side of the playground on the side of boundary line;<br>– the defending player – at the line dividing the playground into two zones, face to attacking players (fig. 1).<br><br><br>**Fig. 1**<br>5m<br>3m<br>12m<br>⊢— 10m —⊣ | – the attacking player without the ball should move at a maximum speed to the area behind the defending player's back;<br>– the attacking players with the ball and without it should act simultaneously;<br>– the defending player should responded timely to the beginning of movement if the attacking player without the ball into the area behind the defending player's back;<br>– the defending player should move backwards at a maximum speed and try to be approx. 3 meters from the opponent;<br>– the defending player should quickly define the direction of sending the ball on the attacking player's way and perform a turn for moving to the ball frontwise; |

## Task 2 continuation

The attacking player suddenly begins to move quickly into the zone 10x12 meters for receiving the ball on a way.

At the beginning of the attacking player's without the ball opening:

– the defending player begins to move back, moving backwards of half-sideways forward;

– the attacking player possessing the ball begins to perform a pass with a kick «from hands by foot» with a mount trajectory into the area behind the defending player's back (fig. 2).

– the defending player should move to the ball frontwise at a maximum speed;

– the attacking player should follow the defending player until the moment he gets the ball beyond the playground

**Fig. 2**

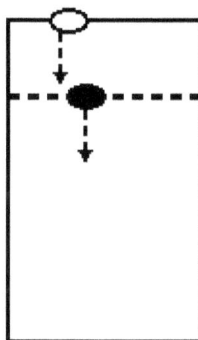

Having defined the direction of a pass on the attacking player's way, the defending player quickly turns, moves to the ball frontwise, come over it and get it beyond the playground through the one of its long sides (fig. 3).

Task 2 continuation

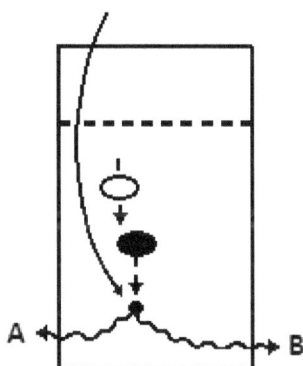

Fig. 3

**Variants:**
a) if players can't perform a pass with a foot with necessary precision, the ball is sent with a hand;
b) points of players' initial position across the width of the pitch are varied (fig. 4)

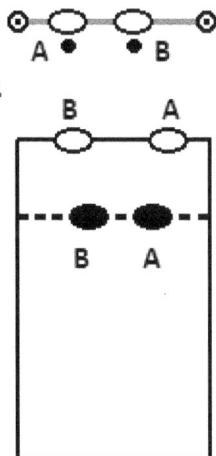

Fig. 4

## Task 3. Knocking out the ball, sent on the attacking player's way into the area behind the defending player's back

| Task description | Requirements for task performance quality |
|---|---|
| Playground 15 meters long and 10 meters wide is marked, divided into 2 zones 5 and 10 meters long.<br>Boundary line 10 meters long is marked opposite to the short side of the playground 5 meters from it.<br>Two attacking and one defending players are situated:<br>– the attacking player with the ball – at the short side of the playground on the side of boundary line;<br>– the attacking player without the ball – at boundary line;<br>– the defending player – at the line dividing the playground into two zones, face to attacking players (fig. 1).<br><br><br><br>**Fig. 1** | – the attacking player without the ball should move at a maximum speed to the area behind the defending player's back;<br>– the attacking players with the ball and without it should act simultaneously;<br>– the defending player should timely begin to move back with consideration for the speed of the attacking player's movement and try to be approx. 3 meters from the opponent;<br>– the defending player should quickly define the direction of sending the ball on the attacking player's way and move to the ball;<br>– the defending player shouldn't allow the attacking player to touch the ball sent on his way, and the ball to touch the pitch surface; |

Task 3 continuation

| | |
|---|---|
| The attacking player suddenly begins to move quickly into the zone 10x15 meters for receiving the ball on a way. At the moment when the attacking player without the ball reaches the playground: <br> – the defending player begins to move back, moving backwards of half-sideways forward; <br> – the attacking player possessing the ball begins to perform a pass with a hand with a mount trajectory into the area behind the defending player's back (fig. 2). | – the attacking player should move to the ball until the moment when the defending player knocks the ball out, but act not with a maximum activity |

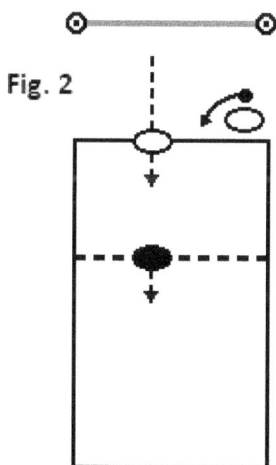

Fig. 2

Having defined the direction of sending the ball on the attacking player's way, the defending player moves to the ball and without allowing it to touch the surface of the pitch, knocks it with a head or a foot through one of long sides of the playground or in zone 5x10 meters (fig. 3).

Task 3 continuation

**Fig. 3**

**Variants:**
a) directions of sending the ball on the attacking player's way are varied;
b) points of players' initial position across the width of the pitch are varied (fig. 4)

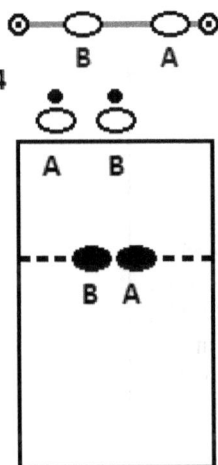

**Fig. 4**

# 4. 5. Drills for learning actions while passing the ball at the attacking player's foot or on his way

**Task 1. Restraint of the attacking player's attempt to come over the ball after a lengthwise pass at foot or on a way and get over the defending player's zone of responsibility along the length of the pitch**

| Task description | Requirements for task performance quality |
|---|---|
| Playground 17 meters long and 10 meters wide is marked, divided into 2 zones 5 and 12 meters long. Boundary line 10 meters long is marked opposite to the short side of the playground 3 meters from it. Two attacking and one defending players are situated: <br> – the attacking player with the ball – at boundary line; <br> – the attacking player without the ball – in zone 5x10 meters; <br> – the defending player – in the playground 3 meters from the attacking player without the ball from the side opposite relative to the attacking player with the ball, face to attacking players (fig. 1). On signal the attacking player without the ball begins to move along the playground for receiving the ball at his foot or on a way from the partner, changing the direction of movement and using dummies. | – the attacking player without the ball should move for receiving the ball at a maximum speed; <br> – while controlling the attacking player without the ball, the defending player should be approx. 3 meters away from him before the moment of sending the ball to this player and see actions of the attacking player possessing the ball with that; <br> – the attacking player possessing the ball should timely sent it to a partner at foot or on a way depending on situation; |

Task 1 continuation

**Fig. 1**

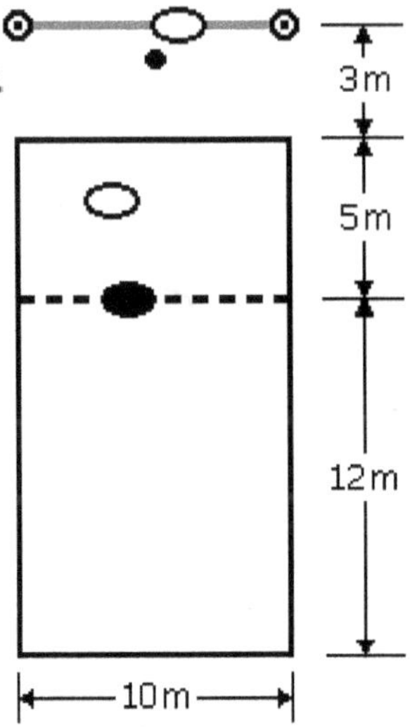

3m

5m

12m

|← 10m →|

While controlling actions of the attacking player, the defending player moves so that to be approx. 3 meters from him all the time up to the moment of sending the ball to him.

The attacking player possessing the ball sends it to a partner with a kick «from hands by foot» over the pitch surface at foot in the closest zone of the playground or with a mounted trajectory on a way to the distant zone of the playground into the area behind the defending player's back.

The attacking player tries to come over the ball and get it through the side of the playground, distant relative to boundary line, beyond it (fig. 2).

If the attacking player comes over the ball after a pass at foot, he gets 1 point, and if in the area behind the defending player's back – 3 points.

– the defending player should anticipate the moment and the direction of a pass by the attacking player on his preparative actions to a pass performance and beginning of strike motion;

– the defending player should timely respond to the beginning of movement of the attacking player without the ball into the area behind the defending player's back, and exclude the possibility of a successful pass on the attacking player's way in principle by moving back;

– during sending the ball on the attacking player's way the defending player should always be first on the ball;

– when the ball is sent at the attacking player's foot, the defending player should move forward at a maximum speed for interception of the ball, and in failing to do so perform an active tackling along the playground

Task 1 continuation

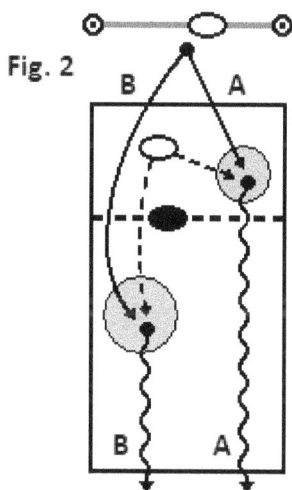

Fig. 2

If the attacking player gets the ball through the short side of the playground, distant relative to boundary line, beyond it, he gets 1 point.

The defending player tries to prevent the attacking player from getting the ball through the short side of the playground, distant relative to boundary line, beyond it, solving two issues with that.

The main issue is to prevent the opponent from coming over the ball in the area behind the defending player's back, timely moving back (fig. 3A).

When sending the ball at the attacking player's foot the defending player should try to intercept the ball, and in failing to do so go in tackle (fig. 3B).

If the defending player intercepts the ball sent on the attacking player's way, he gets 2 points, and if at foot – 1 point.

Task 1 continuation

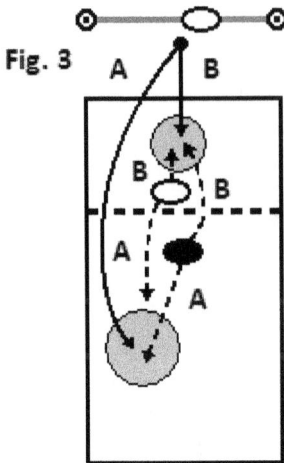

Fig. 3

If the defending player tackles the ball from the attacking player or knocks it out beyond the playground while tackling, he gets 1 point.
**Offsides are not given.**
The duration of one task repetition is no longer than 10 seconds.
**Variants:**
a) if players can't perform a pass with a foot with necessary precision, the ball is sent with a hand;
b) points of players' initial position across the width of the pitch are varied

## Task 2. Restraint of the attacking player's attempt to come over the ball after pass at foot or on a way and get over the defending player's zone of responsibility along the length of the pitch

| Task description | Requirements for task performance quality |
|---|---|
| The playground 15 meters long and 12 meters wide is marked. Boundary line 12 meters long is marked opposite to the short side of the playground 10 meters away from it.<br>Two attacking and one defending players are situated:<br>– the attacking player with the ball – outside the playground 3 meters from its long side opposite to its middle;<br>– the attacking player without the ball – at boundary line;<br>– the defending player – at the short side of the playground near to boundary line (fig. 1). 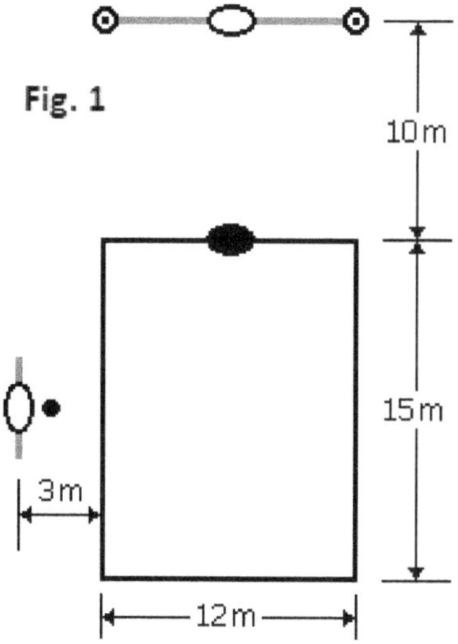 | – the attacking player without the ball should vary the direction of movement into the playground;<br>– the attacking player without the ball should move for receiving the ball at a maximum speed;<br>– while controlling the attacking player without the ball, the defending player should be approx. 3 meters away from him before the moment of sending the ball to this player and see actions of the attacking player possessing the ball with that;<br>– the attacking player possessing the ball should timely sent it to a partner at foot or on a way depending on situation; |

Fig. 1

10 m

15 m

3 m

12 m

25

## Task 2 continuation

On signal the attacking player without the ball begins to move into the playground for receiving the ball at his foot or on a way from the partner, changing the direction of movement and using dummies.

While controlling actions of the attacking player, the defending player moves so that to be approx. 3 meters from him all the time up to the moment of sending the ball to him.

The attacking player possessing the ball sent it to his partner with a foot over the pitch surface at foot or on a way into the area behind the defending player's back.

The attacking player tries to come over the ball and get it through the side of the playground, distant relative to boundary line, beyond it (fig. 2).

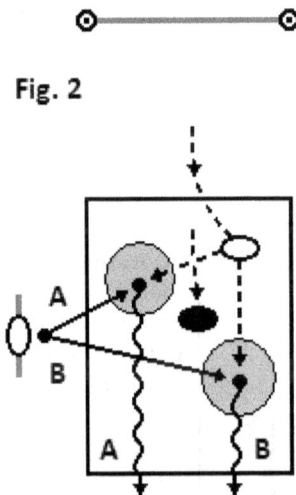

**Fig. 2**

– the defending player should anticipate the moment and the direction of a pass by the attacking player on his preparative actions to a pass performance and beginning of strike motion;

– the defending player should timely respond to the beginning of movement of the attacking player without the ball into the area behind the defending player's back, and exclude the possibility of a successful pass on the attacking player's way in principle by moving back;

– during sending the ball on the attacking player's way the defending player should always be first on the ball;

– when the ball is sent at the attacking player's foot, the defending player should move forward at a maximum speed for interception of the ball, and in failing to do so perform an active tackling along the playground

Task 2 continuation

If the attacking player comes over the ball after a pass at foot, he gets 1 point, and if in the area behind the defending player's back – 3 points.

If the attacking player gets the ball through the short side of the playground, distant relative to boundary line, beyond it, he gets 1 point.

The defending player tries to prevent the attacking player from getting the ball through the short side of the playground, distant relative to boundary line, beyond it, solving two issues with that.

The main issue is to prevent the opponent from coming over the ball in the area behind the defending player's back, timely moving back (fig. 3).

**Fig. 3**

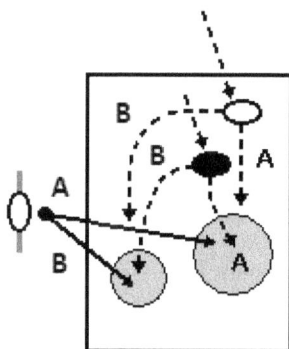

Task 2 continuation

When sending the ball at the attacking player's foot the defending player should try to intercept the ball, and in failing to do so go in tackle (fig. 4).

**Fig. 4**

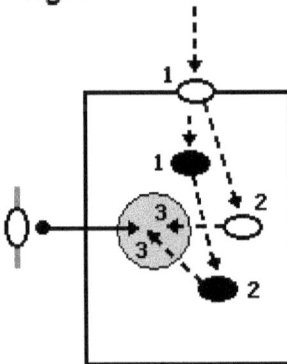

If the defending player intercepts the ball sent on the attacking player's way, he gets 2 points, and if at foot – 1 point.

If the defending player tackles the ball from the attacking player or knocks it out beyond the playground while tackling, he gets 1 point.

**Offsides are not given.**

The duration of one task repetition is no longer than 10 seconds.

**Variant:** points of initial players' position are varied across the width of the pitch (the attacking player with the ball is situated at the other long side of the playground)

## Task 3. Restraint of the attacking player's attempt to shoot on goal from the defending player's zone of responsibility after a diametral pass at foot or on a way

| Task description | Requirements for task performance quality |
|---|---|
| The playground 16 meters long and 12 meters wide is marked. Goal is mounted on one short side of the playground, and boundary line 12 meters long is marked on the other 4 meters from it. Boundary line 16 meters long is marked opposite to the long side of the playground 8 meters from it. Goalkeeper gets into position in goal. Two attacking and one defending players are situated: <br> – the attacking player with the ball – at boundary line 16 meters long; <br> – the attacking player without the ball – at boundary line 12 meters long; <br> – the defending player – at the short side of the playground 4 meters away from the attacking player without the ball (fig. 1). <br><br> <br> Fig. 1 <br> 4 m <br> 16 m <br> 8 m <br> 12 m | – the attacking player without the ball should vary the direction of movement into the playground; <br> – the attacking player without the ball should move for receiving the ball at a maximum speed; <br> – while controlling the attacking player without the ball, the defending player should be 1-3 meters away from him before the moment of sending the ball to this player depending on his position relative to the goal and see actions of the attacking player possessing the ball with that; <br> – the attacking player possessing the ball should timely sent it to a partner at foot or on a way depending on situation; |

## Task 3 continuation

On signal the attacking player without the ball begins to move into the playground for receiving the ball at his foot or on a way from the partner, changing the direction of movement and using dummies.

While controlling actions of the attacking player, the defending player moves so that to be approx. 2-3 meters from him all the time up to the moment of sending the ball to him.

The attacking player possessing the ball sent it to his partner with a foot at foot or on a way into the area behind the defending player's back.

The attacking player tries to shoot on goal:

a) necessarily with a first touch;
b) after handling the ball (fig. 2).

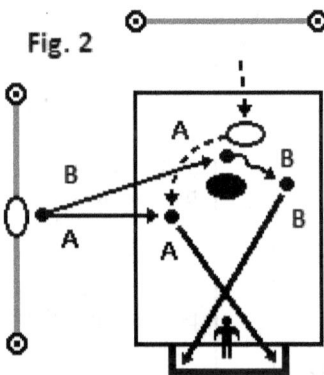

Fig. 2

The attacking player tries to prevent the attacking player from shooting on goal, solving two issues with that.

– the defending player should anticipate the moment and the direction of a pass by the attacking player on his preparative actions to a pass performance and beginning of strike motion;

– the defending player should timely respond to the beginning of movement of the attacking player without the ball into the area behind the defending player's back, and exclude the possibility of a successful pass on the attacking player's way in principle by moving back;

– during sending the ball on the attacking player's way the defending player should always be first on the ball;

– during sending the ball on the attacking player's way the defending player should knock the ball while falling if necessary;

The main issue is to prevent the opponent from shooting on goal from the area behind the defending player's back, timely moving back (fig. 3A).

When sending the ball at the attacking player's foot the defending player should try to intercept the ball, and in failing to do so block the shoot or go in tackle depending on the attacking player's actions (fig. 3B).

– when the ball is sent at the attacking player's foot, the defending player should move forward at a maximum speed for interception of the ball, and in failing to do so block the shot or perform an active tackling, if the attacking player decides to shot on goal after handling the ball

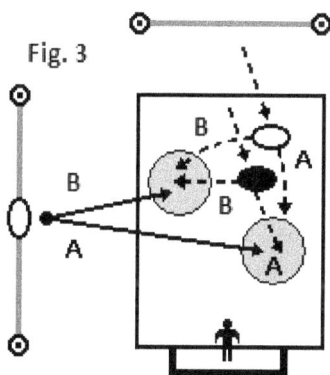

Fig. 3

**Offsides are not given.**
The duration of one task repetition is no longer than 4-5 seconds.
**Variants:**
a) points of initial players' position are varied across the width of the pitch (the attacking player with the ball is situated at the other long side of the playground);
b) points of initial position of the attacking player with the ball along the length of the pitch

# 4. 6. Drills for learning actions while pressing the attacking player out towards the half-way line

**Task 1. Going forward when the attacking player with the ball is back to the goal, moving back and knocking the ball sent into the goal behind the defending player's back**

| Task description | Requirements for task performance quality |
|---|---|
| The playground 15 meters long and 10 meters wide is marked. Goal 6x2 meters is mounted on the short side of the playground.<br>One attacking and one defending player are situated:<br>– the attacking player with the ball – beyond the playground at its short side distant relative to the goal face to the goal;<br>– the defending player – at the goal-line in the middle of the goal face to the attacking player (fig. 1).<br>On the first signal the attacking player makes a U-turn with the ball. Right after the attacking player gets into position back to the goal, the defending player begins to move to him quickly (fig. 2).<br>When the defending player gets forward at 8-10 meters, the second signal follows for the attacking player. | – right after the attacking player with the ball gets into position back to the goal, the defending player should begin to move forward and stop timely relative to the beginning of performing a U-turn to the goal by the attacking player;<br>– the defending player should not begin to move back untimely, i.e. at the moment when the attacking player with the ball has just begun performing a U-turn to the goal;<br>– the attacking player should send the ball into the net with a mounted trajectory with a shot of medium power and not with a powerful shot with a linear trajectory; |

Task 1 continuation

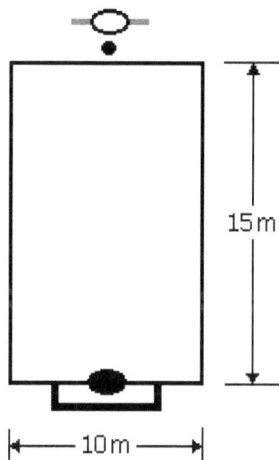

Fig. 1

15 m

|←——— 10 m ———→|

– the defending player should anticipate the moment and the direction of a pass by the attacking player on his preparative actions to a pass performance and beginning of strike motion;

– the defending player should quickly define the direction of the ball sent into the net and knock it out, preventing from crossing the goal-line

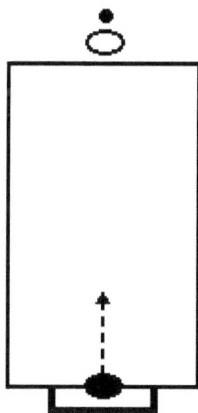

Fig. 2

On the second signal the attacking player should turn face to the goal, prepare the ball to a pass with a second touch and send it with a mounted trajectory into the net with a third with a medium speed from the outside of the playground.

Task 1 continuation

The defending player stops moving froward, when the attacking player begin to turn face to the goal (fig. 3).

**Fig. 3**

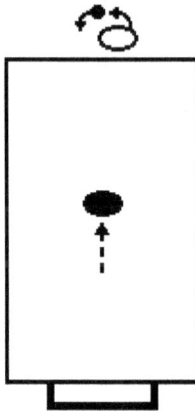

When the attacking player begins to perform a pass, the defending player begins to move back, moving backwards or half-sideways forward (fig. 4).

**Fig. 4**

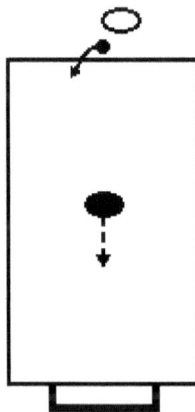

Task 1 continuation

Having defined the direction of the ball sent into the net, the defending player moves to the ball in the area at the goal and, having prevented it from crossing the goal-line, knocks it with a head or a foot through one of long sides of the playground or with a mounted trajectory towards the attacking player (fig. 5).

Fig. 5

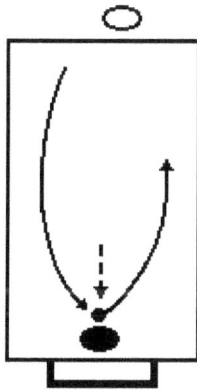

**Variants:**
a) points of initial players' position across the width of the pitch are varied (opposite and diagonally to each other);
b) speed of performance of preparative actions for sending the ball into the bet by the attacking player (successive touches of the ball come one after another without a delay or with some delay between the first and the second touches and between the second and the third touches)

## Task 2. Going forward when the ball moves to the attacking player, moving back and knocking out the ball sent into the net behind the defending player's back

| Task description | Requirements for task performance quality |
|---|---|
| The playground 15 meters long and 10 meters wide is marked. Goal 6x2 meters is mounted on the short side of the playground.<br>One attacking player, one defending player and one assistant are positioned:<br>– the attacking player – beyond the playground at its short side distant relative to the goal;<br>– the defending player – at the goal-line in the middle of the goal face to the attacking player;<br>– the assistant with the ball – at the goal-line alongside of it face to the attacking player (fig. 1).<br><br><br>Fig. 1    15 m    10 m | – right after the performance of a pass by the assistant the defending player should begin moving forward and stop timely relative to the distance between the ball and the attacking player;<br>– the defending player should not begin to move back untimely, i.e. at the moment when the ball flying to the attacking player is still at sufficiently long distance from him;<br>– the attacking player should send the ball into the net with a mounted trajectory with a shot of medium power and not with a powerful shot with a linear trajectory;<br>– the defending player should anticipate the moment and the direction of a pass by the attacking player on his preparative actions to a pass performance and beginning of strike motion; |

Task 2 continuation

| | |
|---|---|
| The assistant sends the ball to the attacking player with a foot over the pitch surface or with a mounted trajectory.<br>Right after the assistant performs a pass, the defending player begins to move quickly towards the attacking player. Up to the moment when the ball appears in close vicinity to the attacking player the defending player stops moving forward (fig. 2). | – the defending player should quickly define the direction of the ball sent into the net and knock it out, preventing from crossing the goal-line |

**Fig. 2**

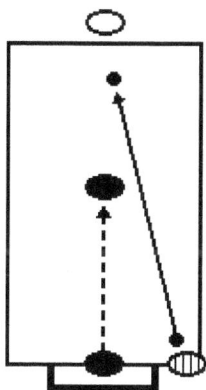

The attacking player receives the ball and sends it with a first touch without a delay with a mounted trajectory into the net with a medium speed from the outside of the playground.

When the attacking player begins to perform a pass, the defending player begins to move back, moving backwards or half-sideways forward (fig. 3).

Task 2 continuation

**Fig. 3**

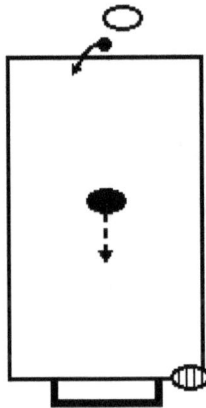

Having defined the direction of the ball sent into the net, the defending player moves to the ball in the area at the goal and, having prevented it from crossing the goal-line, knocks it with a head or a foot through one of long sides of the playground or with a mounted trajectory towards the attacking player (fig. 4).

**Fig. 4**

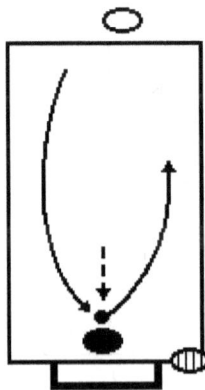

Task 2 continuation

**Variants:**
a) points of players' initial position across the width of the pitch are varied;
b) at initial position the assistant is situated at 15-20 meters from the attacking player so that to perform diametral passes to him from the left and right (fig. 5 and 6)

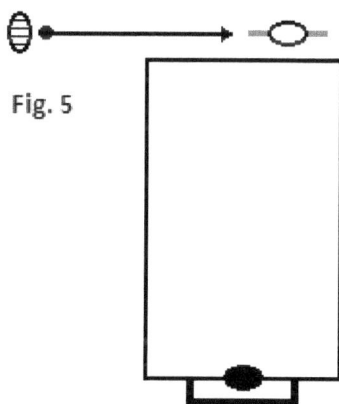

Fig. 5

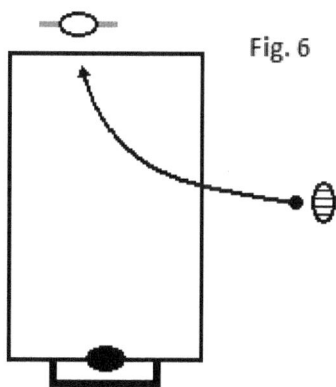

Fig. 6

**Task 3. Going forward when the ball is moving to the attacking player, moving back and knocking out the ball sent to the area behind the defending player's back, on another attacking player's way, who has left an offside**

| Task description | Requirements for task performance quality |
|---|---|
| The playground 15 meters long and 10 meters wide is marked. Goal 6x2 meters is mounted on the short side of the playground.<br>Two attacking and one defending players are situated:<br>– the attacking player of a back line (APBL) – beyond the playground at its short side distant relative to the goal;<br>– the attacking player of a front line (APFL) with the ball – at the goal-line alongside of it face to the partner;<br>– the defending player – at the goal-line in the middle of the goal face to the attacking player (fig. 1). 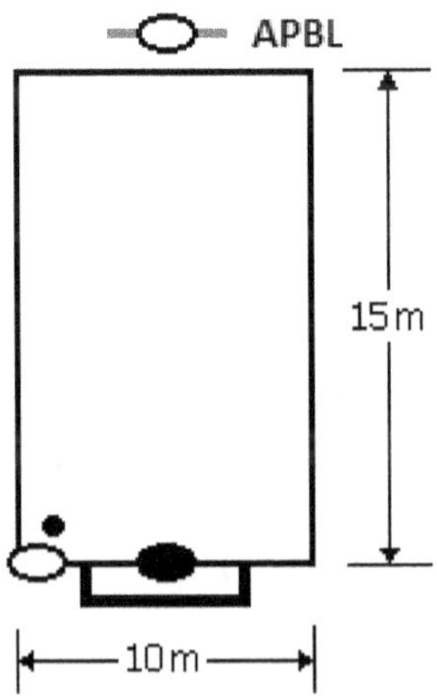 | – right after the performance of a pass by the attacking player of a front line the defending player should begin moving forward and stop timely relative to the distance between the ball and the attacking player of a back line;<br>– the attacking player of a front line should not delayed the beginning of leaving an offside;<br>– after the attacking player of a front line has left an offside the defending player should quickly take such position that this player was approx. 3 meters in front of him;<br>– the defending player should not begin to move back untimely, i.e. at the moment when the ball flying to the attacking player of a back line is still at sufficiently long distance from him; |

Fig. 1

Task 3 continuation

The attacking player of a front line sends the ball to the attacking player of a back line with a foot over the pitch surface or with a mounted trajectory.

Right after the attacking player of a front line has performed a pass, the defending player begins to move quickly towards the attacking player of a back line. Up to the moment when the ball appears in close vicinity to this player the defending player stops moving forward.

Right after the defending player has begun going forward the attacking player begins to move quickly towards the position of the attacking player of a back line and leaves an offside (fig. 2).

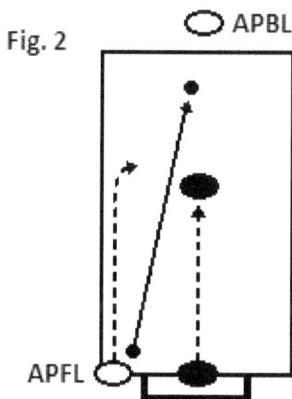

Fig. 2

APBL

APFL

The attacking player of a back line receives the ball and gets ready to perform a pass.

– the attacking player of a front line should vary the direction of movement into the area behind the defending player's back;

– the attacking player of a front line should move at a maximum speed to the area behind the defending player's back;

– the attacking player of a back line should send the ball into the net with a mounted trajectory with a shot of medium power and not with a powerful shot with a linear trajectory;

– the defending player should anticipate the moment and the direction of a pass by the attacking player of a back line on his preparative actions to a pass performance and beginning of strike motion;

– the defending player should quickly define the direction of the ball sent into the net and knock it out, preventing from crossing the goal-line, and the attacking player – from touching the ball;

Task 3 continuation

| | |
|---|---|
| Once the attacking player of a front line leaves an offside, the defending player quickly takes such position that this player was approx. 3 meters in front of him.<br><br>The attacking player of a front line begins to move quickly to the area behind the defending player's back for receiving the ball on a way.<br><br>When the attacking player of a front line begins to open:<br>– the defending player begins to move back, moving backwards of half-sideways forward;<br>– the attacking player of a back line begins to perform a pass with a mounted trajectory into the net with a medium speed from the outside of the playground so that the attacking player of a front line can touch it in the area behind the defending player's back (fig. 3). | – the attacking player should move to the ball until the moment when the defending player knocks the ball out, but act not with a maximum activity |

Fig. 3

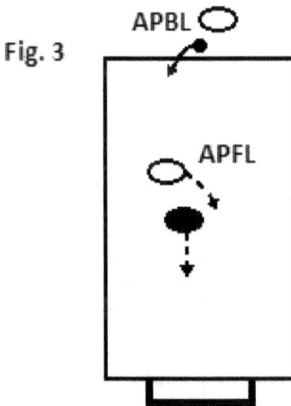

Task 3 continuation

Having defined the direction of the ball sent into the net, the defending player moves to the ball in the area at the goal and, having prevented it from crossing the goal-line, and the attacking player from touching the ball, knocks it with a head or a foot through one of long sides of the playground or with a mounted trajectory towards the attacking player of a back line (fig. 4).

APBL ⬭

**Fig. 4**

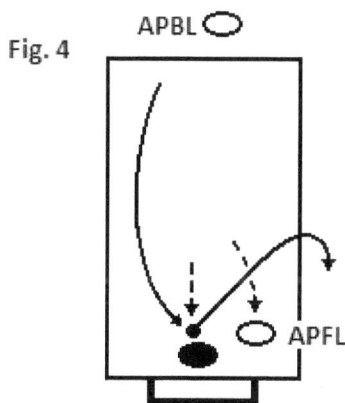

○ APFL

Offsides are given only until the moment when the attacking player of a front line leaves an offside.
**Variants:**
a) points of players' initial position across the width of the pitch are varied;
b) directions in which the attacking player of a front line leaves an offside relative to the defending player are varied

**Task 4. Going forward when the ball is moving to the attacking player, moving back and knocking out the ball sent into the area behind the defending player's back on a way to the another attacking player moving from the deep**

| Task description | Requirements for task performance quality |
|---|---|
| The playground 15 meters long and 10 meters wide is marked. Goal 6x2 meters is mounted on the short side of the playground.<br>Two attacking and one defending players are situated:<br>– right attacking player (RAP) and left attacking player (LAP) – beyond the playground at its short side distant relative to the goal few meters from each other;<br>– the defending player with the ball – at the goal-line in the middle of the goal face to the attacking players (fig. 1). 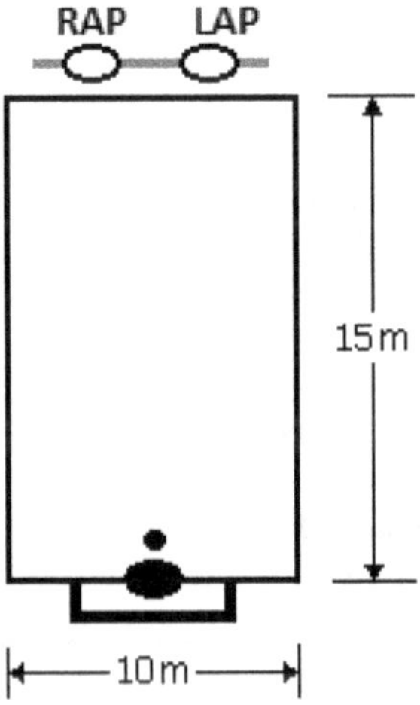 | – right after the performance of a pass to one of the attacking players the defending player should begin moving forward and stop timely relative to the distance between the ball and this attacking player;<br>– the attacking players with the ball and without it should act simultaneously;<br>– the defending player should not begin to move back untimely, i.e. at the moment when the ball flying to one of attacking players is still at sufficiently long distance from this player;<br>– the defending player should responded timely to the beginning of movement if the attacking player without the ball into the area behind the defending player's back; |

Fig. 1

RAP  LAP

15 m

10 m

Task 4 continuation

The defending player sends the ball to one of attacking players with a foot over the pitch surface or with a mounted trajectory.

Right after a pass the defending player begins quickly move towards attacking players. Up to the moment when the ball appears in close vicinity to one of attacking players the defending player stops moving forward (fig. 2).

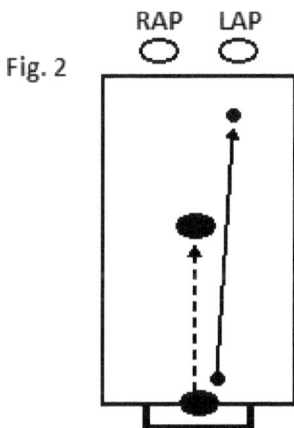

RAP  LAP

Fig. 2

Right of left attacking player receives the ball and gets ready to perform a pass.

Once one of attacking players receives the ball, another begins to move quickly to the area behind the defending player's back, for receiving the ball on a way.

– the attacking player without the ball should vary the direction of movement into the area behind the defending player's back;

– the attacking player without the ball should move at a maximum speed to the area behind the defending player's back;

– the attacking player should send the ball into the net with a mounted trajectory with a shot of medium power and not with a powerful shot with a linear trajectory;

– the defending player should anticipate the moment and the direction of a pass by the attacking player on his preparative actions to a pass performance and beginning of strike motion;

– the defending player should quickly define the direction of the ball sent into the net and knock it out, preventing from crossing the goal-line, and the attacking player – from touching the ball;

Task 4 continuation

| | |
|---|---|
| When the attacking player without the ball begins to open:<br>– the defending player begins to move back, moving backwards of half-sideways forward;<br>– the attacking player possessing the ball begins to perform a pass with a mounted trajectory into the net with a medium speed from the outside of the playground so that the partner can touch it in the area behind the defending player's back (fig. 3). | – the attacking player should move to the ball until the moment when the defending player knocks the ball out, but act not with a maximum activity |

Fig. 3

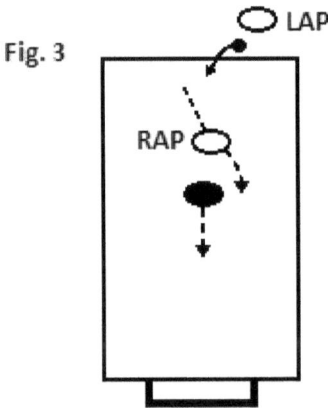

Having defined the direction of the ball sent into the net, the defending player moves to the ball in the area at the goal and, having prevented it from crossing the goal-line, and the attacking player from touching the ball, knocks it with a head or a foot through one of long sides of the playground or with a mounted trajectory towards the attacking player who has performed a pass (fig. 4).

Task 4 continuation

Fig. 4

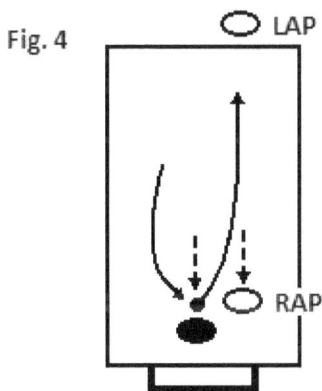

**Offsides are not given.**
**Variants:**
a) directions of movement of the attacking player without the ball into the area behind the defending player's back;
b) points of the defending player's initial position across the width of the pitch and direction of his passes are varied (fig. 5)

Fig. 5

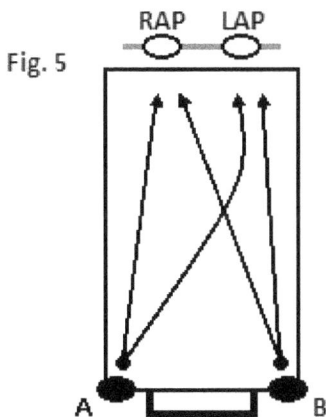

# CHAPTER 5.
# DEFENDING PLAYERS' LEARNING OF ACTIONS IN «TWO ON ATTACKING PLAYER WITHOUT THE BALL SITUATED IN FRONT OF THEM ALONG THE LENGTH OF THE PITCH» SITUATIONS

## 5. 1. Tasks and emphasis of the work

While learning the defensive play in «two on the attacking player without the ball situated in front of them along the length of the pitch» it is necessary to learn footballers three main kinds of shared actions.

**First.** To control the opponent not possessing the ball in «their shared zone of responsibility».

**Second.** To prevent attacking player's attempts to possess the ball after a pass at his foot or on his way.

**Third.** To press the attacking player out towards the halfway line.

In the course of learning these actions the attention is focused on development of players' abilities and skills of psychomotor character as follows:

– to «transfer» the attacking player under partner's control in cases of this player switching from one defending player's «zone of responsibility» to another;

– to define actions priority while restraint of attacking player's attempts to receive the ball;

– to cover each other at attempts to intercept the ball sent to the attacking player.

With those actions to the left and to the right by each of defending players is the most effective methodological technique.

# 5. 2. Drills for learning actions as a couple while controlling the attacking player in shared zone of responsibility

**Task 1. Controlling the attacking player without the ball as a couple during his movements to the left and to the right**

| Task description | Requirements for task performance quality |
|---|---|
| Four limited areas 1x1 meter are marked at the same line at a distance:<br>– between first and second, third and fourth – 4 meters;<br>– between second and third – 6 meters.<br>The corridor 16 meters long and 1 meter wide is marked in parallel to limited areas 3 meters from them. Three balls are mounted in the corridor: one in the middle and two other at the ends of the corridor.<br>One attacking and two defending players are situated:<br>– the attacking player – in the middle of the corridor face to limited areas;<br>– the left defending player (LDP) – in the second limited area face to the attacking player;<br>– the right defending player (LDP) – in the third limited area face to the attacking player (fig. 1).<br>On signal the attacking player begins to move through the corridor to the left and to the right to one of the balls, changing the direction of movement and using dummies. | – the attacking player should touch the ball 3-4 times, moving along the corridor;<br>– the attacking player should use all possible ways (vary speed and direction of movement, simulate touching the ball) to that defending players do not get in time to take corresponding positions to the moment he touches the ball;<br>– defending players should react to changes in the attacking player's actions at a maximum speed;<br>– defending players should try to act in strict compliance with the attacking player's actions; |

Task 1 continuation

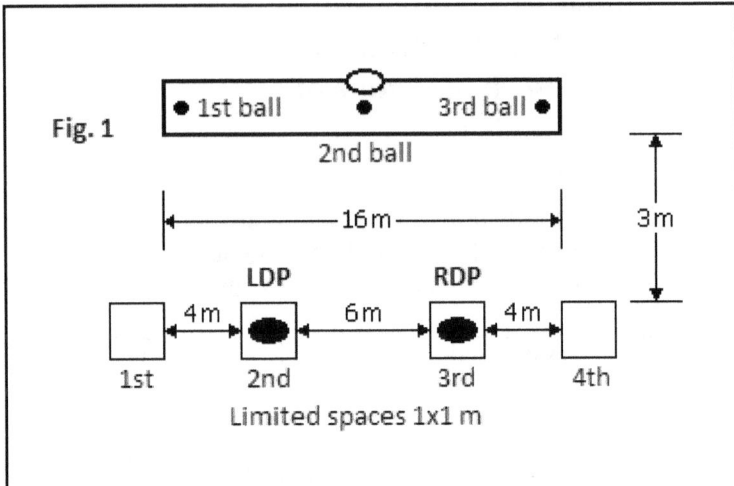

Fig. 1

While performing moving along the corridor for a few seconds, the attacking player should touch the ball (the same or different ones) with both hands 3-4 times, without observing some strict sequence.

Defending player try to control the attacking player, moving simultaneously to the left and to the right so that at the moment when the opponent touches:

– the first ball – the left defending player is in the first limited area, and the right defending player – in the second (fig. 2);

– the second ball – the left defending player is in the second limited area, and the right defending player – in the third (fig. 3);

– the third ball – the left defending player is in the third limited area, and the right defending player – in the fourth (fig. 4).

– while performing movements defending players should not turn their back to the attacking player;

– while moving, defending players should not be stiff-legged, but slightly bent in the knees;

– while moving, defending players should work with legs quickly

Task 1 continuation

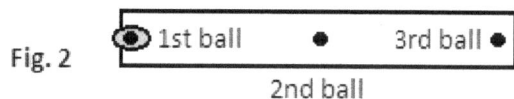

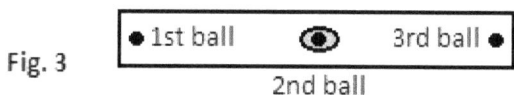

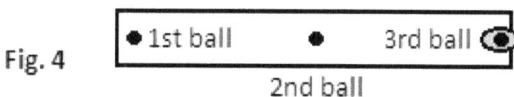

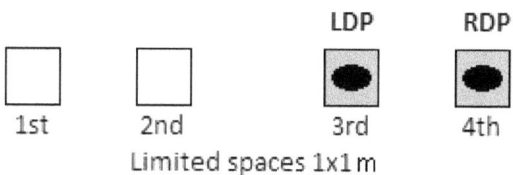

**Fig. 2**

1st ball        2nd ball        3rd ball

LDP        RDP

1st        2nd        3rd        4th

Limited spaces 1x1 m

**Fig. 3**

1st ball        2nd ball        3rd ball

LDP        RDP

1st        2nd        3rd        4th

Limited spaces 1x1 m

**Fig. 4**

1st ball        2nd ball        3rd ball

LDP        RDP

1st        2nd        3rd        4th

Limited spaces 1x1 m

Task 1 continuation

| Each time defending players succeed to do so, they get a point.<br>If at least one of defending players is not both legs in corresponding limited area at the moment when the attacking player touches some ball, the attacking player gets a point (fig. 5 and 6).<br>The duration of one task repetition is no longer than 10 seconds | |

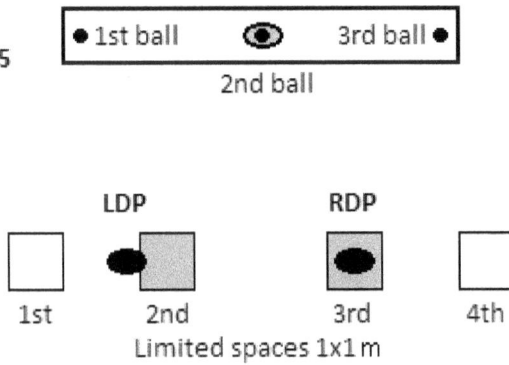

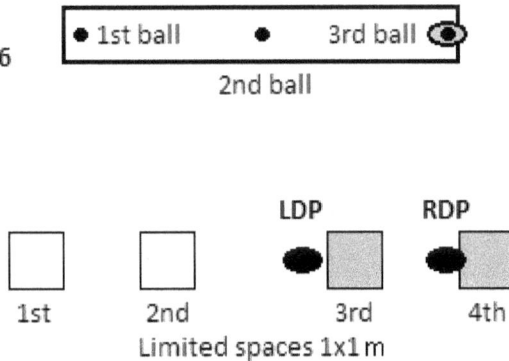

## Task 2. Controlling the attacking player without the ball as a couple during his movements back and fourth

| Task description | Requirements for task performance quality |
|---|---|
| Four boundary lines 10 meters long are marked in parallel to each other at 3 meters. Three flat constraints are mounted on each first, second and third boundary lines: one in the middle and two other at the ends of the boundary line.<br>One attacking and two defending players are situated:<br>– the attacking player – at the middle of the second boundary line face to the third boundary line;<br>– the left defending player (LDP) and the right defending player (RDP) – at the third boundary line 2 meters from its ends and 6 meters from each other face to the attacking player (fig. 1). | – the attacking player should touch the ball 3-4 times, moving between the first and the third boundary lines;<br>– the attacking player should use all possible ways (vary speed and direction of movement, simulate touching the ball) to that defending players do not get in time to take corresponding positions to the moment he touches the ball; |

**Fig. 1**

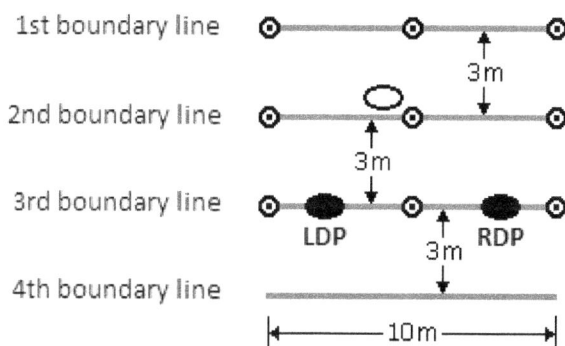

87

Task 2 continuation

| | |
|---|---|
| On signal the attacking player begins to move back and forth between the first and the third boundary lines to one of flat constraints, changing the direction of movement and using dummies. While performing movement between the first and the third boundary lines in any direction (at any angle relative to boundary lines) for a few seconds, the attacking player should touch the flat constraint (the same or different ones) with both hands 3-4 times, without observing some strict sequence. Defending player try to control the attacking player, moving simultaneously back and forth so that at the moment when the opponent touches:<br>– any flat constraint mounted on the first boundary line, they are on the second boundary line (fig. 2);<br>– any flat constraint mounted on the second boundary line, they are on the third boundary line (fig. 3);<br>– any flat constraint mounted on the third boundary line, they are on the fourth boundary line (fig. 4);<br>Each time defending players succeed to do so, they get a point. If at least one of defending players is not both legs on the corresponding boundary line at the moment when the attacking player touches some flat landmark , the attacking player gets a point (fig. 5 and 6). The duration of one task repetition is no longer than 10 seconds | – defending players should react to changes in the attacking player's actions at a maximum speed;<br>– defending players should try to act in strict compliance with the attacking player's actions;<br>– while performing movements, defending players should try to be on a level relative to boundary lines and keep distance between them 6 meters;<br>– while moving, defending players should not be stiff-legged, but slightly bent in the knees;<br>– while moving, defending players should work with legs quickly |

Task 2 continuation

**Fig. 2**

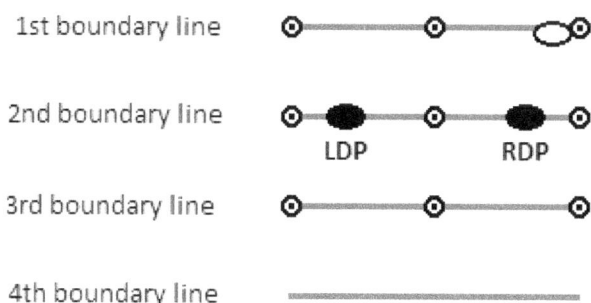

**Fig. 3**

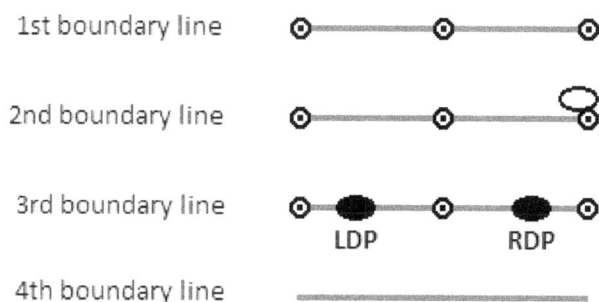

**Fig. 4**

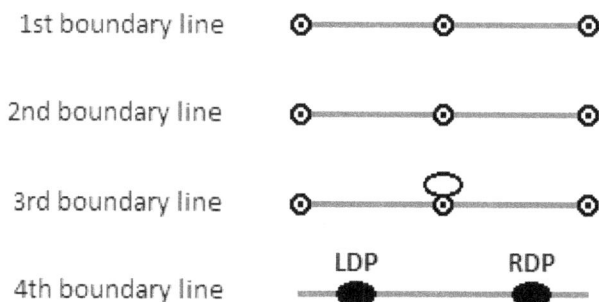

## Task 2 continuation

**Fig. 5**

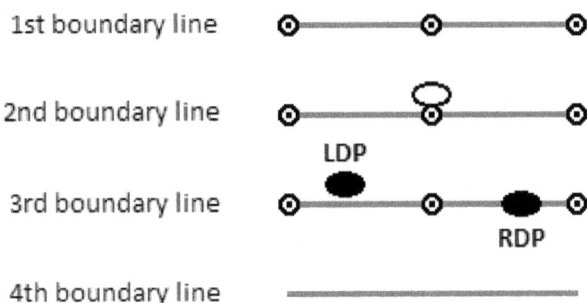

    1st boundary line

    2nd boundary line

    3rd boundary line

    4th boundary line

**Fig. 6**

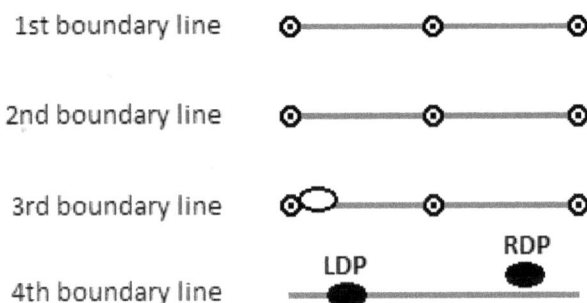

    1st boundary line

    2nd boundary line

    3rd boundary line

    4th boundary line

# 5. 3. Drills for learning actions as a couple in case of pass at the attacking player's foot

**Task 1. One defending player's outcome for interception of the ball sent at the attacking player's foot, and slip of another defending player towards a partner for closing the cleared space**

| Task description | Requirements for task performance quality |
|---|---|
| Two limited areas 2 meters in diameter are marked 8 meters from one another. Boundary line 12 meters long is marked in parallel to limited areas at 3 meters, in the middle of which the limited area 2x1 meters is marked. Three attacking and two defending players are situated: – the attacking player of a back line (APBL) with the ball – 10 meters from the line where limited areas 2 meters in diameter from the side opposite relative to boundary line face to it; – the right attacking player (RAP) and the left attacking player (LAP) – in limited areas 2 meters in diameter; – the left defending player (LDP) and the right defending player (RDP) – at the boundary line 2 meters from its ends and 8 meters from each other face to attacking players (fig. 1). The attacking player of a back line sends the ball at the right attacking player's foot into limited area 2 meters in diameter over the pitch surface. | – while controlling actions of the attacking player without the ball, defending players should be near boundary line up to the moment of sending the ball to this player and see actions of the attacking player of a back line with that; – defending players should anticipate the moment and the direction of a pass by the attacking player of a back line on his preparative actions to a pass performance and beginning of strike motion; |

Task 1 continuation

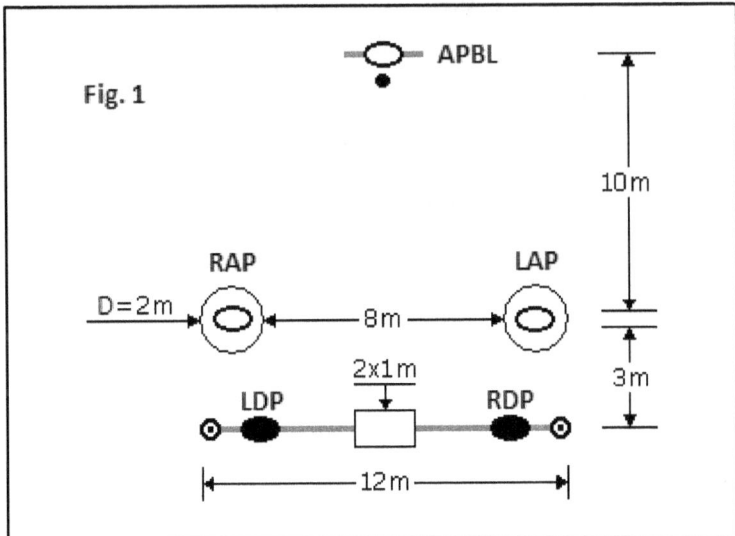

Fig. 1

At the moment of pass performance the left defending player abruptly goes forward, closes with the right attacking player and stops directly close to him.

The right attacking player receives the ball without leaving the limited area.

After the left attacking player begins to go forward, the right defending player begins to move towards his partner so that to take a position in the limited area 2x1 meters at the moment when the former gets near to the right attacking player(fig. 2).

Having received the ball, the right attacking player sends it back to the attacking player of a back line with a second touch after a short pause.

After the attacking player performs a pass to the partner, defending players quickly move to their initial positions (fig. 3).

– the defending player in whose zone of responsibility the attacking player, to whom the attacking player of a back line performs a pass, is situated, should go forward at a maximum speed and closes with the opponent;

– the defending player covering a partner should begin to move towards him right after he begins going forward;

– defending players should get in time to take necessary positions to the moment of ball reception by the right or left attacking player;

Task 1 continuation

Fig. 2

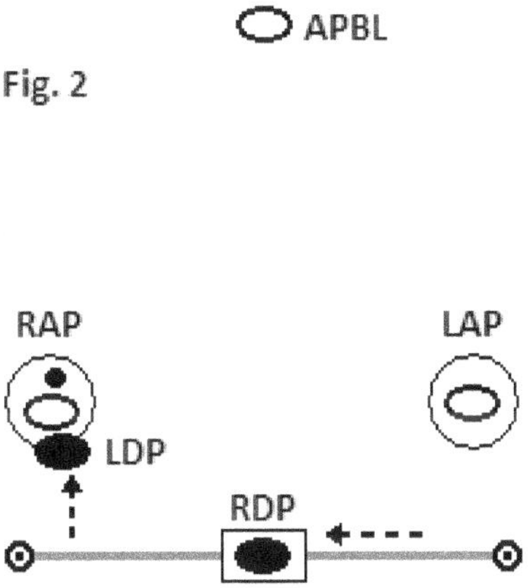

○ APBL

RAP          LAP

LDP

RDP

Fig. 3

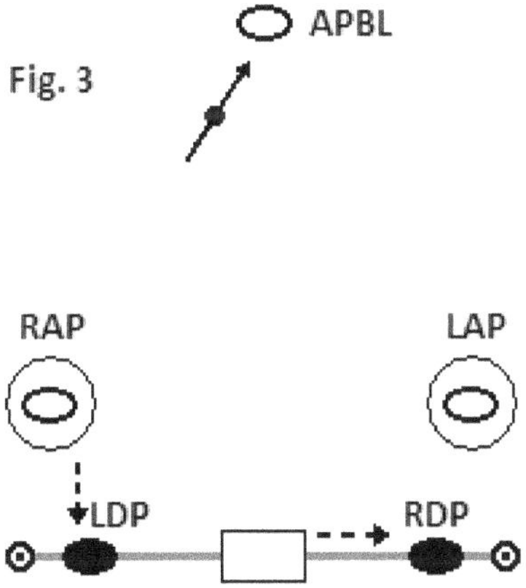

○ APBL

RAP          LAP

LDP          RDP

– defending players should quickly go back at the initial positions after the right or left attacking player performs a pass back to the attacking player of a back line;
– while going back at the initial positions after the right or left attacking player performs a pass back to the attacking player of a back line, defending players should not turn their back to attacking players;
– defending players should perform the task to both sides simultaneously

Having come over the ball, the attacking player of a back line sends it after a short pause at the left attacking player's foot into limited area 2 meters in diameter over the pitch surface.

Task 1 continuation

At the moment of pass performance the right defending player abruptly goes forward, closes with the left attacking player and stops directly close to him.

The left attacking player receives the ball without leaving the limited area.

After the right attacking player begins to go forward, the left defending player begins to move towards his partner so that to take a position in the limited area 2x1 meters at the moment when the former gets near to the left attacking player (fig. 4).

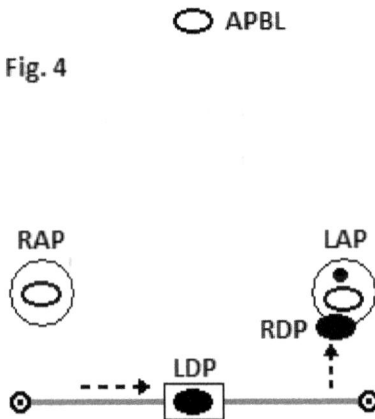

○ APBL

**Fig. 4**

RAP                    LAP

RDP

LDP

Having received the ball, the left attacking player sends it back to the attacking player of a back line with a second touch after a short pause.

After the left attacking player performs a pass to the partner, defending players quickly move to their initial positions (fig. 5).

Task 1 continuation

Fig. 5

○ APBL

RAP                    LAP
◎                      ◎

RDP          LDP
●━━━━[  ]━━━━●

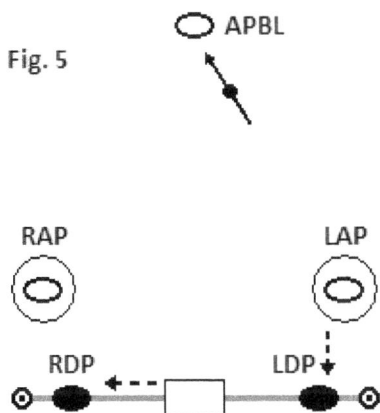

The task is performed 4-5 times in a row to both sides.
**Variants:**
a) speed of sending the ball by attacking players is varied;
b) attacking players perform passes with a second touch without a delay after reception of the ball;
c) if players can't perform a pass with a foot with necessary precision, the ball is sent with a hand;
d) defending players perform the task, having swapped their initial positions

**Task 2. Attacking player's movement across the width of the pitch to the left and to the right for reception of the ball, going out of one defending player for tackling the ball sent at the attacking player's foot and slip of another defending player towards the partner for closing the free space**

| Task description | Requirements for task performance quality |
|---|---|
| The corridor 20 meters long and 2 meters wide is marked. Two zones (left and right) 3 meters long are marked in the corridor 5 meters from its ends. Boundary line 20 meters long is marked in parallel to the corridor at 3 meters. <br> Three goals 2 meters wide, marked with lowly cones, are mounted in parallel to boundary line at 3 meters from the side opposite to the corridor: <br> – one goal (middle) – in point opposite to the middle of boundary line; <br> – two goals (left and right) – in points 5 meters to the left and to the right of the middle goal. <br> One attacking player, two defending players and two assistants are positioned: <br> – the attacking player – in the middle of the corridor face to boundary line; <br> – the left defending player (LDP) and the right defending player (RDP) – at the boundary line 7 meters from its ends and 6 meters from each other face to the corridor; <br> – assistants with balls – at the ends of the corridor beyond it face to the attacking player (fig. 1). | – the attacking player should move to one of the corridor's zones for receiving the ball suddenly and quickly; <br> – defending players should be at boundary line until the moment when the ball is sent to the attacking player; <br> – players' assistants should send the ball to the attacking player timely and precisely at foot; <br> – defending players should anticipate the moment and the direction of a pass by the assistant on his preparative actions to a pass performance and beginning of strike motion; <br> – the defending player, in whose zone of responsibility the attacking player tries to receive the ball, should go forward at a maximum speed and close with the opponent; |

Task 2 continuation

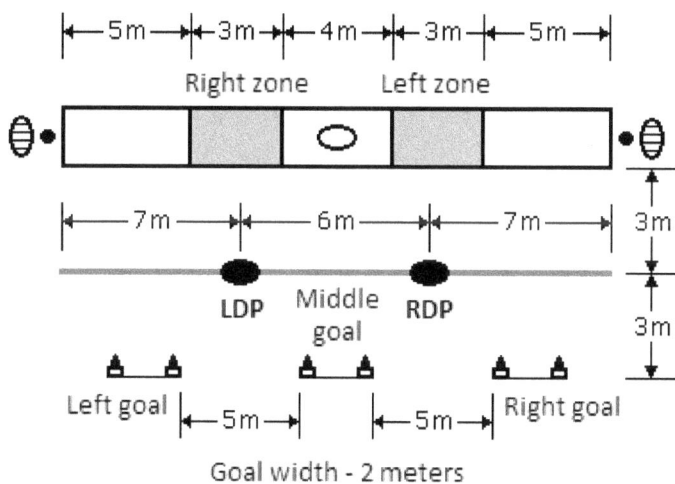

Fig. 1

Goal width - 2 meters

| The attacking player suddenly begins to move quickly into one of marked zones of the corridor.<br>Players' assistant with the ball situated closer to the zone of the corridor where the attacking player has begun to move, sends the ball to him into that zone over the pitch surface.<br>The attacking players tries to send the ball with a first touch or having handled it (with a second or third touch) necessarily from this zone of the corridor over the pitch surface into the middle goal or in the goal closest to the assistant who has performed a pass to the attacking player (fig. 2). | – the defending player covering the partner should begin to move towards him right after he begins to move forward;<br>– the defending player who goes at the attacking player should firstly try to overlap the direction of sending the ball into the goal closer to the assistant who has performed a pass;<br>– the attacking player should try to send the ball into the net quickly; |

Task 2 continuation

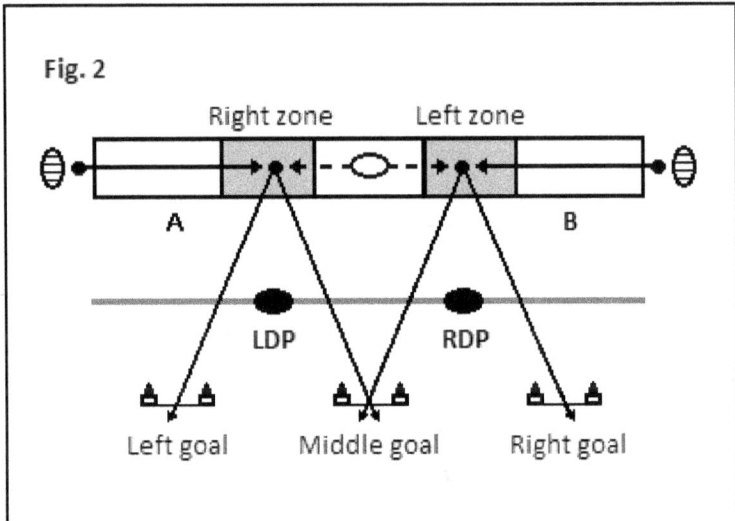

Fig. 2

Right zone    Left zone

A                    B

LDP          RDP

Left goal    Middle goal    Right goal

| If the attacking player begins to move to the right zone of the corridor for reception of the ball, then at the moment of pass performance the left defending player abruptly goes forward and try to prevent the attacking player from sending the ball to the left or middle goal. After the left defending player has begun to move forward, the right defending player begins to move along boundary line towards the partner so that to overlap the direction of sending the ball to the middle goal by the attacking player (fig. 3). If the attacking player begins to move to the left zone of the corridor for reception of the ball, the right defending player goes at him, while the left defending player moves towards the partner to protect the middle goal (fig. 4). | – defending players should get in time to take necessary positions to the moment of ball reception by the attacking player; – defending players should perform the task to both sides simultaneously |

Task 2 continuation

**Fig. 3**

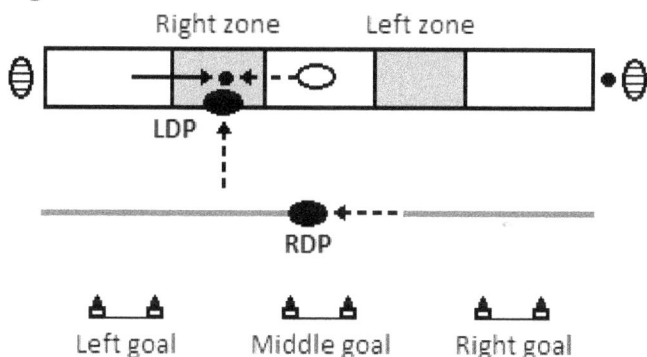

**Fig. 4**

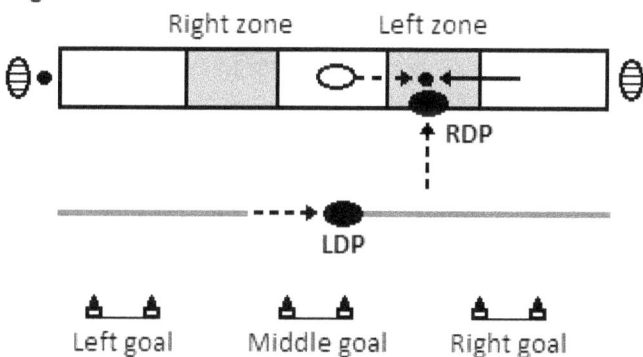

| Variants:<br>a) before starting the movement into one of corridor's zones the attacking player shows the false direction of his movement to defending players, using dummies;<br>b) defending players perform the task, having swapped their initial positions | |

**Task 3. A pass towards the touch-line, going out for tackling the ball by the central or right defending player depending on the area in which the ball is sent, and moving of another defending player towards a partner for closing the free space**

| Task description | Requirements for task performance quality |
|---|---|
| Boundary line 15 meters long is marked. Two limited spaces 3x3 meters are marked in parallel to boundary line at 2 meters: one (right) – opposite to the middle of boundary line, another (left) – opposite to its right end. Three goals 3 meters wide and marked with lowly cones are mounted from the side opposite to points of limited spaces marking in parallel to boundary line at 3 meters: – one goal (middle) – in point opposite to the middle of boundary line; – two goals (left and right) – in points 3 meters to the left and to the right of the middle goal. Two attacking players, two defending players and one assistant are positioned: – the attacking player of a back line (APBL) – in point in the middle of the pitch opposite to the left goal 10 meters from boundary line from the side of limited spaces, face to boundary line; – the attacking player of a front line (APFL) – in the right limited space (situated opposite to the middle on boundary line); – players' assistant – in the left limited space (situated opposite to the right end of boundary line); | – defending players should be at boundary line until the moment when the ball is sent by the attacking player of a back line; – the attacking player of a back line should perform passes without strict sequence and precisely in one of three possible directions; – defending players should anticipate the moment and the direction of a pass by the attacking player of a back line on his preparative actions to a pass performance and beginning of strike motion; – while passing the ball to the right attacking player and to the players' assistant the central defending player and the right defending player respectively should go forward and close with the opponent at a maximum speed; |

Task 3 continuation

| | |
|---|---|
| – the right defending player (RDP) – at boundary line 4 meters away from its right end face to attacking players; <br> – the left defending player (LDP) – at boundary line 4 meters away from its left end face to attacking players (fig. 1). The attacking player of a back line, without observing strict sequence, sends the ball over the pitch surface in one of three directions: <br> a) to the left goal aiming to score a goal; <br> b) to the right limited space to the attacking player of a front line; <br> c) to the left limited space to players' assistant. | – the defending player covering the partner should begin to move towards him right after he begins to move forward; <br> – while going forward, the right defending player should try to overlap the direction of sending the ball into the right or middle goals to the player's assistant; |

**Fig. 1**

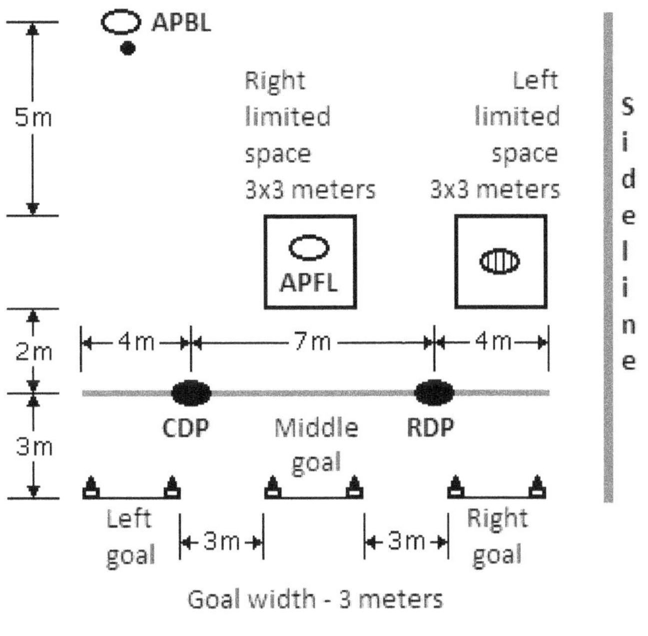

Goal width - 3 meters

## Task 3 continuation

In case of a pass to the attacking player of a front line or players' assistant they try to send the ball from their limited space with a first touch or having tackled it (with a second or a third touch) over the pitch surface into one of the goals (fig. 2).

If the attacking player of a back line sends the ball into the left goal, the central defending player tries to intercept the ball.

If the attacking player of a back line sends the ball to the attacking player of a front line, the central defending player abruptly goes forward at this player and tries to prevent him from sending the ball into the net.

– while going forward, the central defending player should try to overlap the direction of sending the ball into the left or middle goals to the attacking player of a front line;

– the central defending player should be ready for sending the ball into the left goal by the attacking player of a back line;

Fig. 2

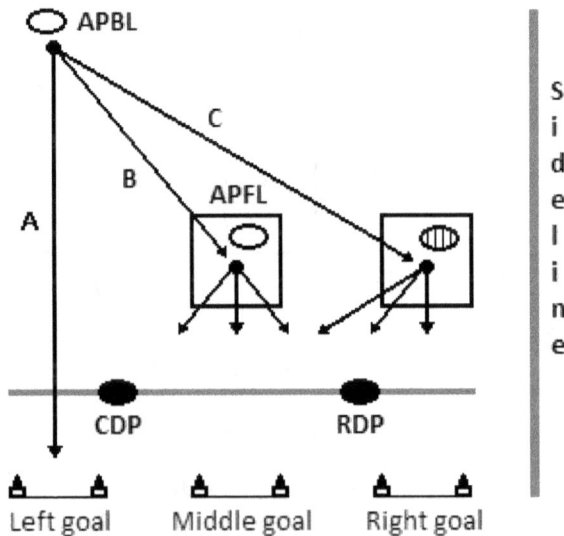

Task 3 continuation

| | |
|---|---|
| After the central defending player has begun to move forward, the right defending player begins to move along boundary line towards the partner so that to overlap the direction of sending the ball to the right and middle goal by the attacking player of a front line (fig. 3). If the attacking player of a back line sends the ball to the players' assistant, the right defending player abruptly goes forward at this player and tries to prevent him from sending the ball into the net. After the right defending player has begun to move forward, the central defending player begins to move along boundary line towards the partner so that to overlap the direction of sending the ball to the middle and left goal by the players' assistant (fig. 4). | – defending players should get in time to take necessary positions to the moment of ball reception by the attacking player of a front line or the players' assistant; – defending players should perform the task to both sides simultaneously |

Fig. 3

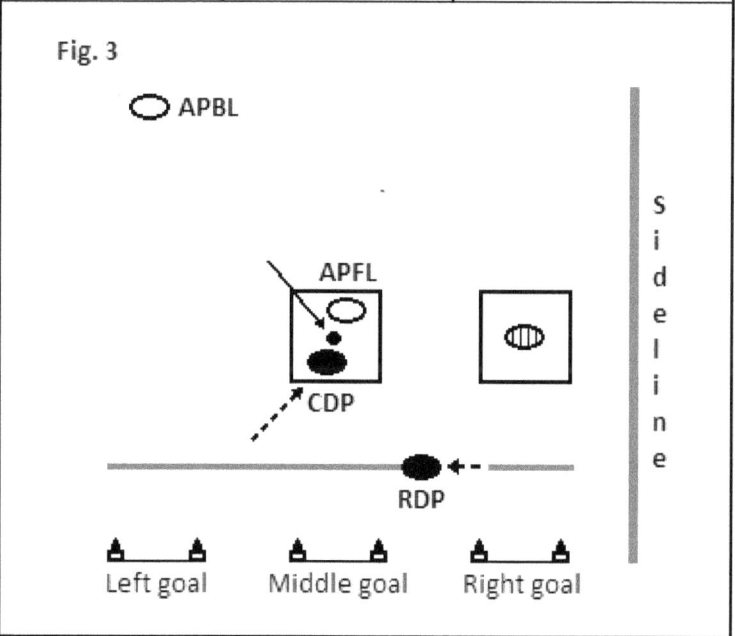

APBL

APFL

CDP

RDP

Side line

Left goal    Middle goal    Right goal

Task 3 continuation

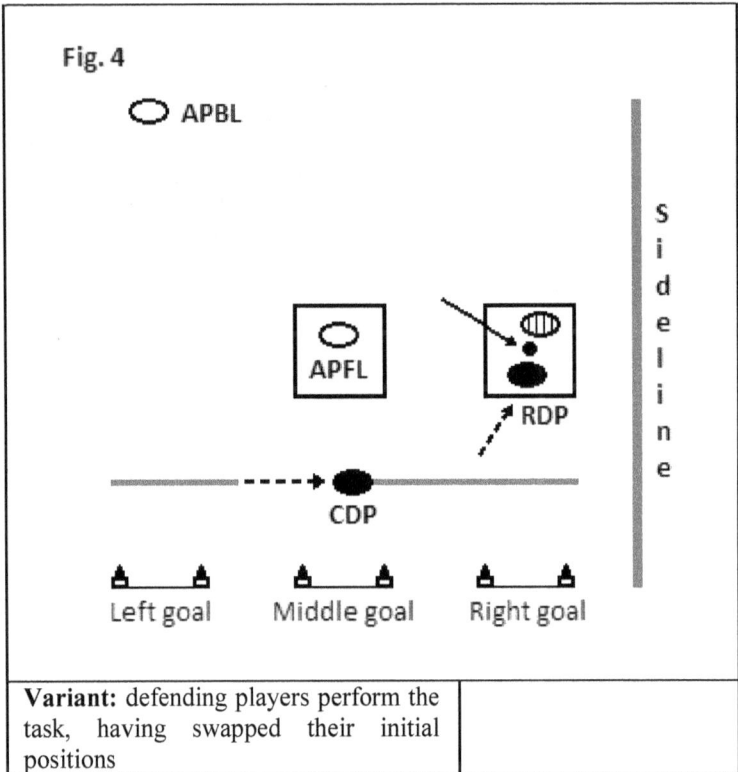

Fig. 4

APBL

APFL

RDP

CDP

Left goal    Middle goal    Right goal

sideline

| Variant: defending players perform the task, having swapped their initial positions | |
|---|---|

**Task 4. A pass from the touch-line, going out for tackling the ball by the central defending player regardless of the area in which the ball is sent, and slip of another defending player towards the partner for closing the free space**

| Task description | Requirements for task performance quality |
|---|---|
| Boundary line 15 meters long is marked. Two limited spaces 3x3 meters are marked in parallel to boundary line at 2 meters: one (right) – opposite to the middle of boundary line, another (left) – opposite to its right end. Three goals 3 meters wide and marked with lowly cones are mounted from the side opposite to points of limited spaces marking in parallel to boundary line at 3 meters: <br> – one goal (middle) – in point opposite to the middle of boundary line; <br> – two goals (left and right) – in points 3 meters to the left and to the right of the middle goal. <br> Two attacking players, two defending players and one assistant are positioned: <br> – the attacking player of a back line (APBL) – in point at the touch-line opposite to the left goal 10 meters from boundary line from the side of limited spaces, face to boundary line; <br> – the attacking player of a front line (APFL) – in the right limited space (situated opposite to the middle on boundary line); <br> – players' assistant – in the left limited space (situated opposite to the right end of boundary line); <br> – the central defending player (CDP) – at boundary line 4 meters away from its right end face to attacking players; | – defending players should be at boundary line until the moment when the ball is sent by the attacking player of a back line; <br> – the attacking player of a back line should perform passes without strict sequence and precisely in one of three possible directions; <br> – defending players should anticipate the moment and the direction of a pass by the attacking player of a back line on his preparative actions to a pass performance and beginning of strike motion; <br> – while passing the ball to the attacking player of a front line and to the players' assistant the central defending player should go forward and close with the opponent at a maximum speed; |

## Task 4 continuation

| | |
|---|---|
| – the left defending player (LDP) – at boundary line 4 meters away from its left end face to attacking players (fig. 1). The attacking player of a back line, without observing strict sequence, sends the ball over the pitch surface in one of three directions: a) to the left goal aiming to score a goal; b) to the right limited space to the attacking player of a front line; c) to the left limited space to players' assistant. | – the left defending player should begin to move towards the partner right after he begins going forward; – while going forward, the central defending player should try to overlap the direction of sending the ball into the right or middle goals to the attacking player of a front line and the players' assistant; |

**Fig. 1**

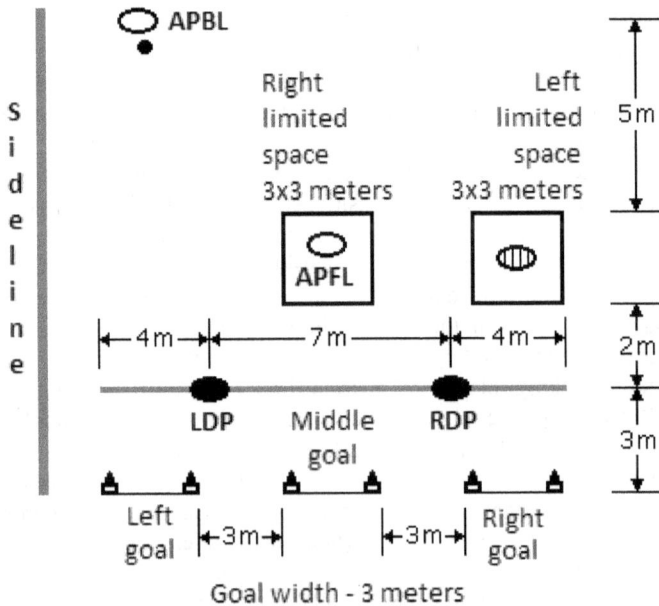

Task 4 continuation

| | |
|---|---|
| In case of a pass to the attacking player of a front line or players' assistant he tries to send the ball from their limited space with a first touch or having tackled it (with a second or a third touch) over the pitch surface into one of the goals (fig. 2). If the attacking player of a back line sends the ball into the left goal, the left defending player tries to intercept the ball. If the attacking player of a back line sends the ball to the attacking player of a front line, the central defending player abruptly goes forward at this player and tries to prevent him from sending the ball into the net. | – the left defending player should be ready for sending the ball into the left goal by the attacking player of a back line; – defending players should get in time to take necessary positions to the moment of ball reception by the attacking player of a front line or the players' assistant; – defending players should perform the task to both sides simultaneously |

**Fig. 2**

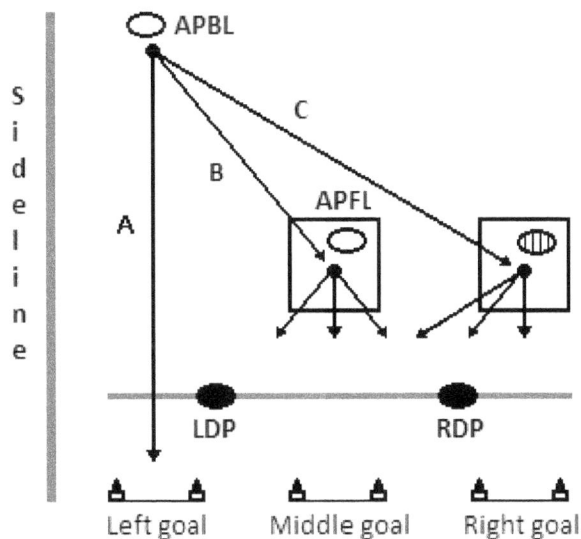

107

Task 4 continuation

After the central defending player has begun to move forward, the left defending player begins to move along boundary line towards the partner so that to overlap the direction of sending the ball to the left and middle goal by the attacking player of a front line (fig. 3).
If the attacking player of a back line sends the ball to the players' assistant, the central defending player abruptly goes forward at this player and tries to prevent him from sending the ball into the net.

**Fig. 3**

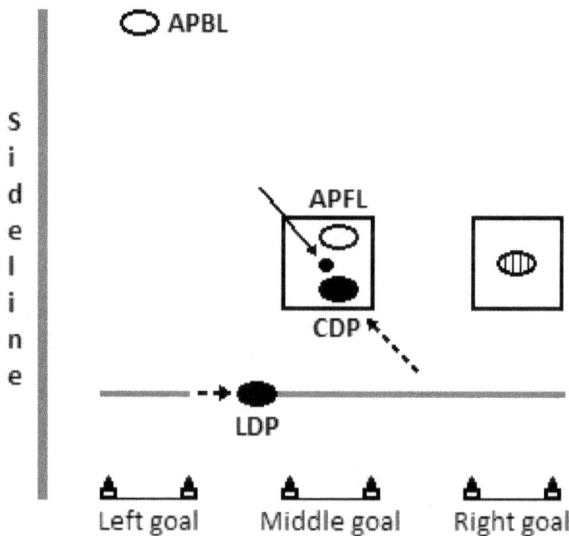

Left goal    Middle goal    Right goal

Task 4 continuation

| After the central defending player has begun to move forward, the left defending player begins to move along boundary line towards the partner so that to overlap the direction of sending the ball to the middle and left goal by the players' assistant (fig. 4). | |

**Fig. 4**

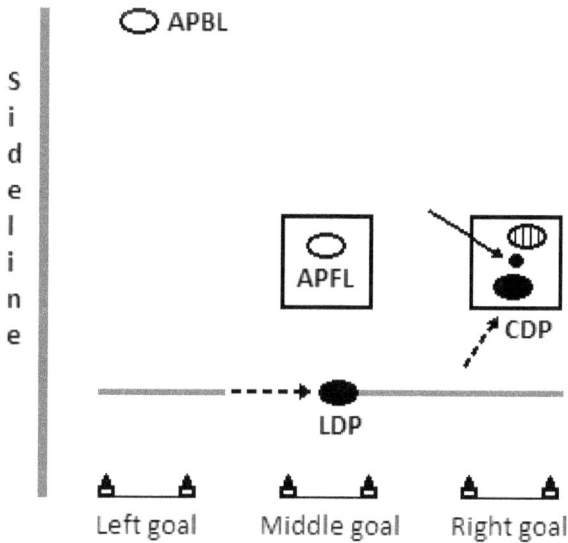

| **Variant:** defending players perform the task, having swapped their initial positions | |

## 5. 4. Drills for learning actions as a couple in case of pass on the attacking player's way

**Task 1. Knocking out the ball sent on the attacking player's way into the area behind defending players back by the defending player, in whose zone of responsibility the ball is sent, and covering the partner by another defending player at the moment of knocking the ball out**

| Task description | Requirements for task performance quality |
|---|---|
| Playground 12 meters long and 16 meters wide is marked, divided into 2 zones 8 meters wide. Boundary line 10 meters long is marked opposite to the long side of the playground 5 meters from it. One attacking and two defending players are situated: – the attacking player with the ball – at boundary line face to the playground; – the right defending player (RDP) and the left defending player (LDP) – at the line bordering the playground across the width and closer to boundary line, 4 meters from its ends and 8 meters from each other face to the attacking player (fig. 1). The attacking player performs a pass by the hand with a mounted trajectory into one of the playground zones. | – defending players should anticipate the moment of a pass by the attacking player on his preparative actions to a pass performance and beginning of strike motion and begin to move back timely; – while moving back defending players should quickly define in which area of the playground the attacking player has sent the ball; – the defending player, in whose zone of responsibility the ball is sent, quickly move to the ball and knock it out, preventing it from touching the surface; |

Task 1 continuation

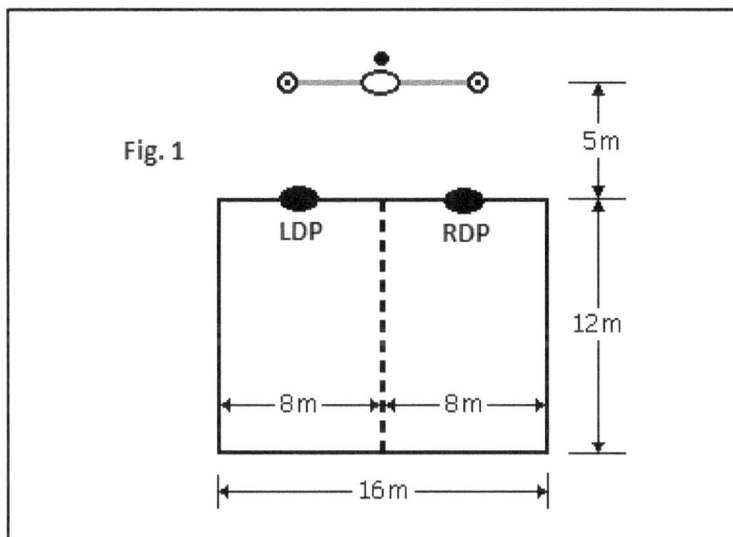

Fig. 1

5m

12m

8m — 8m

16m

When the attacking player begins to perform a pass, defending players begin to move back, moving backwards or half-sideways forward and trying to be approx. in parallel to each other (fig. 2).

Fig. 2

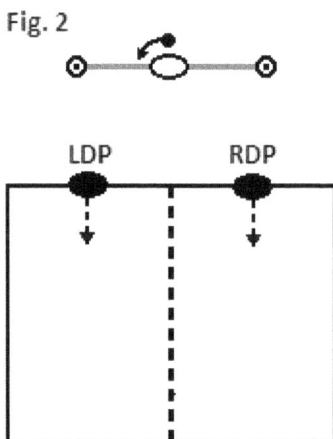

LDP   RDP

– the defending player covering the partner should be approx. 5 meters from the partner and somewhat closer than him to the distant relative to the attacking player long side of the playground at the moment of knocking out the ball by the partner;
– defending players should not be close to each other at the moment when the ball is knocked out by one of them;

Task 1 continuation

| | |
|---|---|
| Having defined the direction of sending the ball; <br> – the defending player, in whose zone of responsibility the ball is sent, moves to the ball and knocks it with a head or a foot without allowing it to touch the pitch surface through one of short sides of the playground or with a mounted trajectory towards the attacking player; <br> – the another defending player moves so that to be approx. 5 meters from the partner and somewhat closer than him to the distant from the attacking player long side of the playground at the moment when the ball is knocked out by the partner (fig. 3). | – the attacking player should send balls into different zones of the playground without strict sequence, varying the height of sending of the ball |

**Fig. 3**

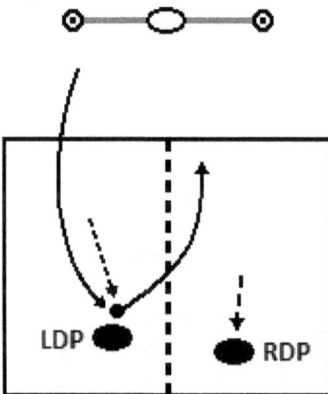

**Variants:**
a) points of the attacking player's initial position at boundary line;
b) defending players perform the task, having swapped their initial positions

**Task 2. Sudden movement of one of
two attacking player into the area behind
the back of the closer to him defending
player, knocking out the ball sent on
the opponent's way by the defending
player, in whose zone of responsibility
the ball is sent, and covering the partner
by another defending players at
the moment of knocking the ball out**

| Task description | Requirements for task performance quality |
|---|---|
| Playground 12 meters long and 16 meters wide is marked, divided into 2 zones 8 meters wide.<br>Boundary line 16 meters long is marked opposite to the long side of the playground 5 meters from it.<br>Two attacking players, two defending players and the assistant are positioned:<br>– the right attacking player (RAP) and the left attacking player (LAP) – at the boundary line 4 meters from its ends and 8 meters from each other face to the playground;<br>– the right defending player (RDP) and the left defending player (LDP) – at the line bordering the playground across the width and closer to boundary line, 4 meters from its ends and 8 meters from each other face to the attacking player;<br>– players' assistant with the ball – at the middle of boundary line face to the playground (fig. 1).<br>One of the attacking players suddenly begins to move into the area behind the back of the defending player closer to him. | – attacking players should move forward for receiving the ball at a maximum speed;<br>– the attacking player trying to receive the ball and the attacking players' assistant should act simultaneously;<br>– defending players should timely react to the beginning of the attacking player's movement and begin to move back;<br>– defending players should quickly move backwards and try to be approx. 3 meters along the length of the pitch from the attacking player moving for reception of the ball; |

Task 2 continuation

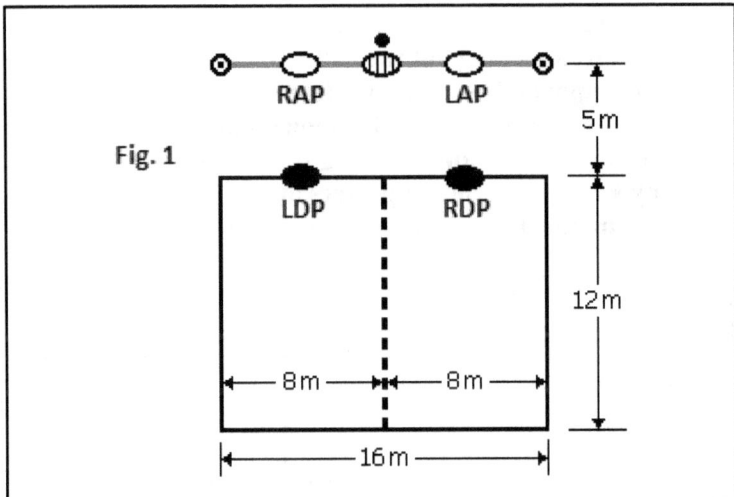

Fig. 1

At the beginning of the attacking player's opening:
– the attacking players' assistant begins to perform a pass with a hand with a mounted trajectory on the attacking player's way;
– defending players begin to move back, moving backwards of half-sideways forward (fig. 2).

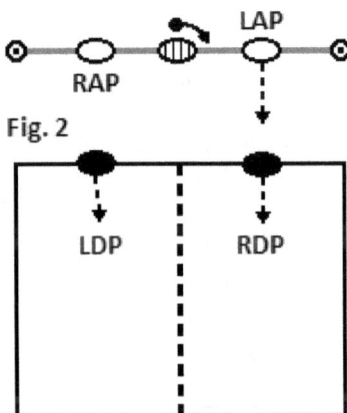

Fig. 2

– while moving back defending players should quickly define in which area of the playground the attacking players' assistant has sent the ball;
– the defending player in whose zone of responsibility the ball is sent should quickly move to the ball and knock it out preventing the attacking player from touching the ball sent on his way, and the ball from touching the pitch surface;

Task 2 continuation

Having defined the direction of sending the ball;
– the defending player, in whose zone of responsibility the ball is sent, moves to the ball and knocks it with a head or a foot without allowing the attacking player to touch the ball through one of short sides of the playground or with a mounted trajectory towards the attacking players' assistant;
– the another defending player moves so that to be approx. 5 meters from the partner and somewhat closer than him to the distant from the attacking players' assistant long side of the playground at the moment when the ball is knocked out by the partner (fig. 3).

– the defending player covering the partner should be approx. 5 meters from the partner and somewhat closer than him to the distant relative to the attacking players' assistant long side of the playground at the moment of knocking out the ball by the partner;
– the attacking player should move to the ball until the moment when the defending player knocks the ball out, but act not with a maximum activity

**Fig. 3**

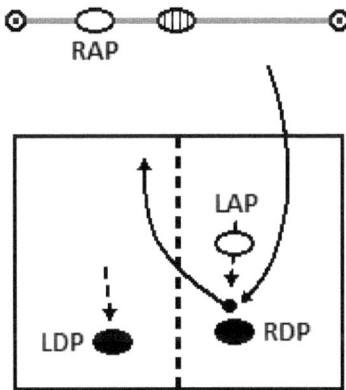

**Variants:**
a) points of attacking players' initial position at boundary line;
b) defending players perform the task, having swapped their initial positions;

Task 2 continuation

c) the attacking player trying to receive the ball may suddenly stop on course of moving, and the attacking players' assistant should pass the ball at his foot in this case.

In such situation the defending player, in whose zone of responsibility the attacking player is positioned, should quickly go at the opponent, trying to get to him as close as possible at the moment when he receives the ball, and another defending player should begin to move towards partner.

If the defending player, in whose zone of responsibility the attacking player is positioned, is more than 3 meters along the length of the pitch at the moment of ball reception by the opponent, then attacking players win in this attempt, and if closer than 3 meters, then winners are defending players (fig. 4)

**Fig. 4**

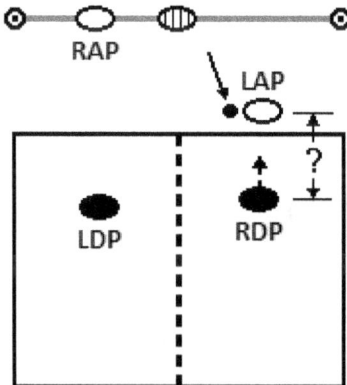

**Task 3. Sudden movement of one of two attacking player into the area behind one or another defending player's back, knocking out the ball sent on the opponent's way by the defending player, in whose zone of responsibility the ball is sent, and covering the partner by another defending players at the moment of knocking the ball out**

| Task description | Requirements for task performance quality |
|---|---|
| Playground 12 meters long and 16 meters wide is marked, divided into 2 zones 8 meters wide.<br>Boundary line 16 meters long is marked opposite to the long side of the playground 5 meters from it.<br>Two attacking players, two defending players and the assistant are positioned:<br>– the right attacking player (RAP) and the left defending player (LAP) – at boundary line ends face to the playground;<br>– the right defending player (RDP) and the left defending player (LDP) – at the line bordering the playground across the width and closer to boundary line, 4 meters from its ends and 8 meters from each other face to the attacking player;<br>– the players' assistant with the ball – at the middle of the line bordering the playground across the width and closer to boundary line (fig. 1).<br>One of attacking players suddenly begins to move into the area behind the defending players' back, maintaining or changing the direction of movement once. | – attacking players should move forward for receiving the ball at a maximum speed;<br>– the attacking player trying to receive the ball and the attacking players' assistant should act simultaneously;<br>– defending players should timely react to the beginning of the attacking player's movement and begin to move back;<br>– defending players should quickly move backwards and try to be approx. 3 meters along the length of the pitch from the attacking player moving for reception of the ball; |

## Task 3 continuation

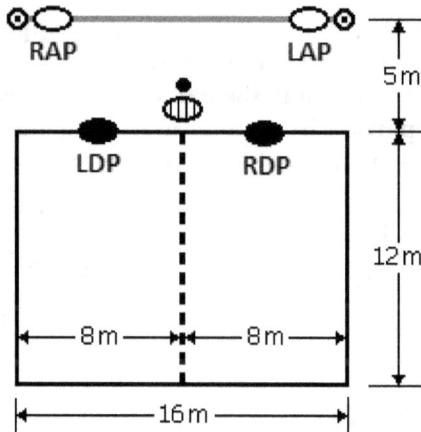

Fig. 1

At the moment when the attacking player begins to open defending players begin to move back, moving backwards of half-sideways forward. Depending on the direction of the opponent's movement they change the direction of movement across the width of the pitch, somewhat close together (fig. 2 and 3).

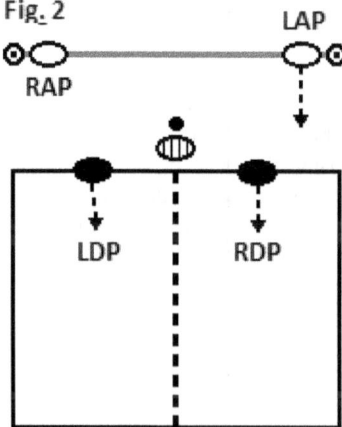

Fig. 2

– while moving back defending players should quickly define in which area of the playground the attacking players' assistant has sent the ball;
– the defending player in whose zone of responsibility the ball is sent should quickly move to the ball and knock it out preventing the attacking player from touching the ball sent on his way, and the ball from touching the pitch surface;

Task 3 continuation

Fig. 3

RAP

LAP

LDP  RDP

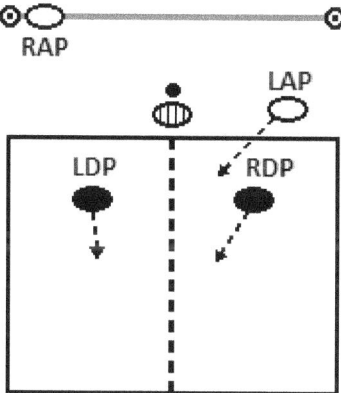

The attacking players' assistant performs a pass with a hand with a mounted trajectory on the attacking player's way into the area of the playground where he has finally decided to move to (fig. 4).

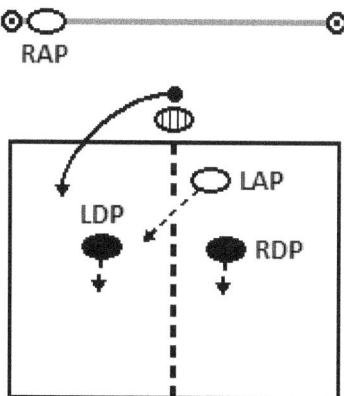

– the defending player covering the partner should be approx. 5 meters from the partner and somewhat closer than him to the distant relative to the attacking players' assistant long side of the playground at the moment of knocking out the ball by the partner;
– the attacking player should move to the ball until the moment when the defending player knocks the ball out, but act not with a maximum activity

Fig. 4

RAP

LAP

LDP

RDP

Task 3 continuation

Having defined the direction of sending the ball;
– the defending player, in whose zone of responsibility the ball is sent, moves to the ball and knocks it with a head or a foot without allowing the attacking player to touch the ball through one of short sides of the playground or with a mounted trajectory towards the attacking players' assistant;
– the another defending player moves so that to be approx. 5 meters from the partner and somewhat closer than him to the distant from the attacking players' assistant long side of the playground at the moment when the ball is knocked out by the partner (fig. 5);

**Fig. 5**

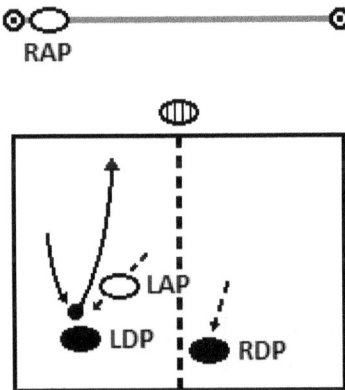

Variants:
a) points of attacking players' initial position at boundary line;
b) defending players perform the task, having swapped their initial positions;

Task 3 continuation

c) the attacking player trying to receive the ball may suddenly stop on course of moving, and the attacking players' assistant should pass the ball at his foot in this case.

In such situation the defending player, in whose zone of responsibility the attacking player is positioned, should quickly go at the opponent, trying to get to him as close as possible at the moment when he receives the ball, and another defending player should begin to move towards partner.

If the defending player, in whose zone of responsibility the attacking player is positioned, is more than 3 meters along the length of the pitch at the moment of ball reception by the opponent, then attacking players win in this attempt, and if closer than 3 meters, then winners are defending players (fig. 6)

Fig. 6

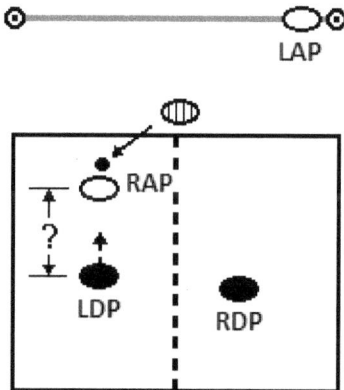

LAP

RAP

LDP

RDP

## 5. 5. Drills for learning actions as a couple in case of pressing the attacking player out towards the half-way line

**Task 1. Going of two defending players forward when the attacking player is positioned with the ball back to them, moving of two defending players back and knocking the ball, sent by the attacking player into one of two goals behind defending players' back, out by one of them**

| Task description | Requirements for task performance quality |
|---|---|
| Playground 15 meters long and 16 meters wide is marked. Two goals 6x2 meters are mounted on the long side 1 meter from the playground corners and 2 meters from each other. One attacking and two defending players are situated: – the attacking player with the ball – beyond the playground at its long side distant relative to the goal face to the goal; – the right defending player (RDP) and the left defending player (LDP) – at the goal-line in the middle of different goals face to the attacking player (fig. 1). On the first signal the attacking player makes a U-turn with the ball. Right after the attacking player gets into position back to the goal, defending players begin to move to him quickly. | – right after the attacking player with the ball gets into position back to the goal, defending players should begin to move forward and stop timely relative to the beginning of performing a U-turn to the goal by the attacking player; – while moving forward, defending players should try to be 7-8 meters from each other and on the same line across the width of the pitch; |

Task 1 continuation

Fig. 1

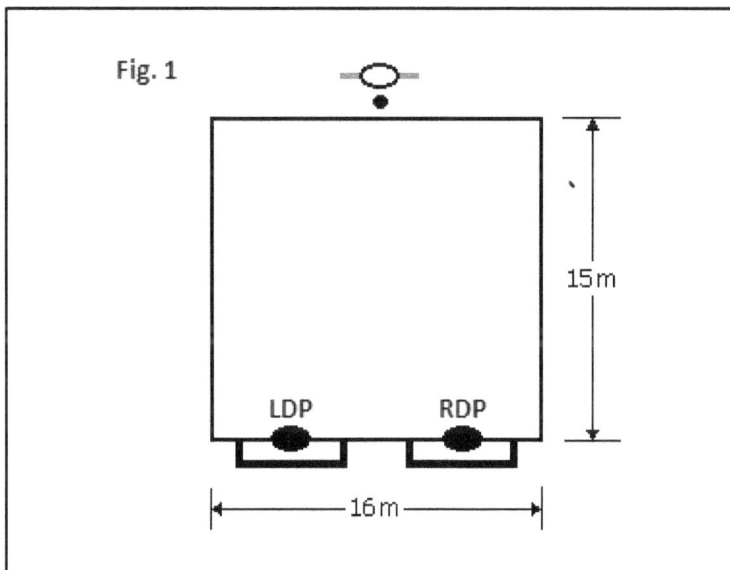

15 m

LDP     RDP

16 m

| | |
|---|---|
| While moving forward, defending players try to be approx. in parallel to each other at 7-8 meters (fig. 2).<br><br>Fig. 2<br><br>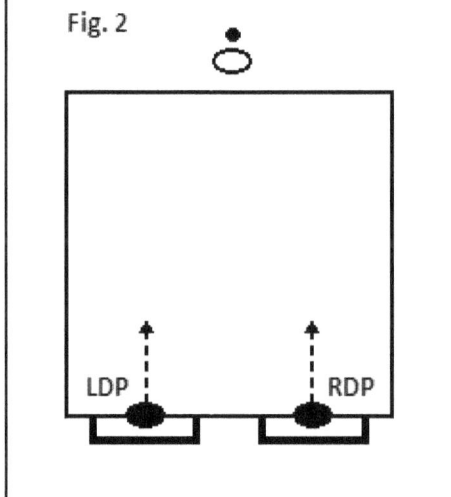<br><br>LDP   RDP | – defending players should not begin to move back untimely, i.e. at the moment when the attacking player with the ball has just begun performing a U-turn to them;<br>– defending players should anticipate the moment of a pass by the attacking player on his preparative actions to a pass performance and beginning of strike motion; |

## Task 1 continuation

When defending players get forward at 8-10 meters, the second signal follows for the attacking player.

On the second signal the attacking player should turn face to the goal, prepare the ball to a pass with a second touch and send it with a mounted trajectory into one of goals with a third with a medium speed from the outside of the playground.

Defending players stop moving forward, when the attacking player begin to turn face to the goal (fig. 3).

**Fig. 3**

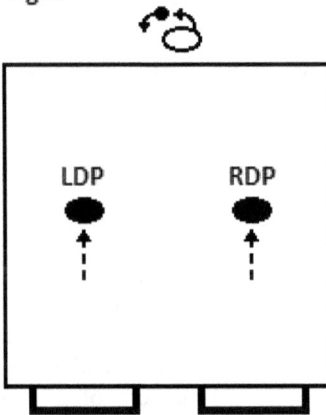

When the attacking player begins to perform a pass into the net, defending players begin to move back, moving backwards or half-sideways forward and trying to be approx. in parallel to each other at 7-8 meters (fig. 4).

– the attacking player should send the ball into the net with a mounted trajectory with a shot of medium power and not with a powerful shot with a linear trajectory;

– while the attacking player performs a pass into the net defending players should move back moving backwards or half-sideways forward up to the moment when they define the direction of the ball;

– defending players should quickly define the direction of the ball sent into the net and knock it out, preventing from crossing the goal-line;

– to the moment when one of defending players knocks out the ball another should be 5-6 meters from him and on the same line across the width of the pitch or somewhat closer to the goal-line

Task 1 continuation

Fig. 4

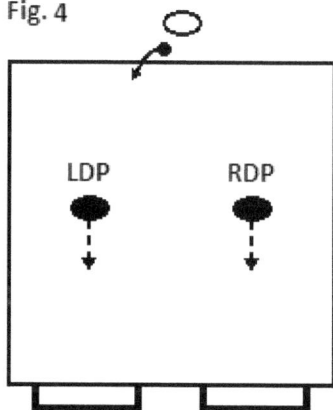

Having defined the direction of the ball, the defending player in whose goal the ball is sent moves to the goal and, having prevented the ball from crossing the goal-line, knocks it with a head or a foot through one of short sides of the playground or with a mounted trajectory towards the attacking player (fig. 5).

Fig. 5

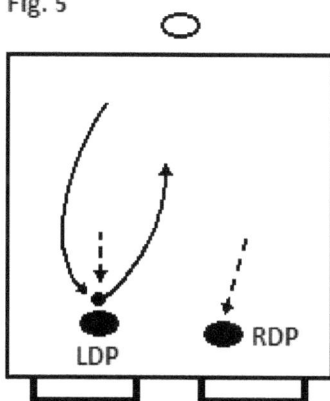

Task 1 continuation

Another defending player moves towards partner so that to be approx. 5-6 meters from him and on the same line across the width of the pitch or somewhat closer to the goal-line to the moment when the partner knocks the ball out.

**Variants:**

a) defending players perform the task, having swapped their initial positions;

b) points of the attacking player's initial position across the width of the pitch are varied (fig. 6)

**Fig. 6**

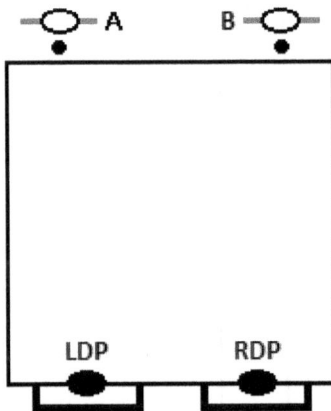

c) speed of performance of preparative actions for sending the ball into the bet by the attacking player (successive touches of the ball come one after another without a delay or with some delay between the first and the second touches and between the second and the third touches)

**Task 2. Pass back to the attacking player, two defending players' moving forward while the ball is moving to the attacking player, two defending players' moving back and knocking out the ball, sent by the attacking player into one of two goals behind defending players' back, by one of them**

| Task description | Requirements for task performance quality |
|---|---|
| Playground 15 meters long and 16 meters wide is marked. Two goals 6x2 meters are mounted on the long side 1 meter from the playground corners and 2 meters from each other.<br>One attacking player, two defending players and one assistant are positioned:<br>– the attacking player – beyond the playground at its long side distant relative to the goal approx. in the middle of the playground;<br>– the right defending player (RDP) and the left defending player (LDP) – at the goal-line in the middle of different goals face to the attacking player;<br>– the assistant with the ball – at the goal-line at the playground corner beyond it face to the attacking player (fig. 1).<br>The assistant sends the ball to the attacking player with a foot over the pitch surface or with a mounted trajectory.<br>Right after the assistant performs a pass defending players begin quickly move towards the attacking player. | – right after the performance of a pass by the assistant defending players should begin moving forward simultaneously and stop timely relative to the distance between the ball and the attacking player;<br>– while moving forward, defending players should try to be 7-8 meters from each other and on the same line across the width of the pitch;<br>– defending players should not begin to move back untimely, i.e. at the moment when the ball flying to the attacking player is still at sufficiently long distance from him;<br>– defending players should anticipate the moment of a pass by the attacking player on his preparative actions to a pass performance and beginning of strike motion; |

Task 2 continuation

Fig. 1

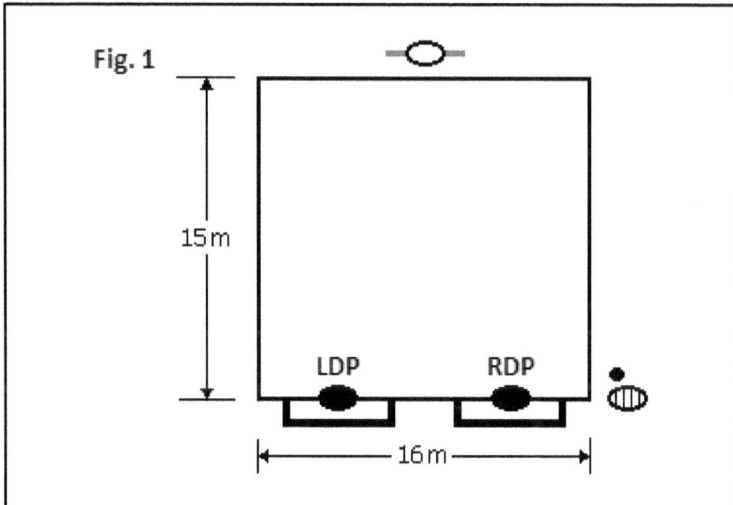

15 m

16 m

LDP    RDP

While moving forward, defending players try to be approx. in parallel to each other at 7-8 meters. To the moment when the ball appears in close vicinity to the attacking player defending players stop moving forward (fig. 2).

Fig. 2

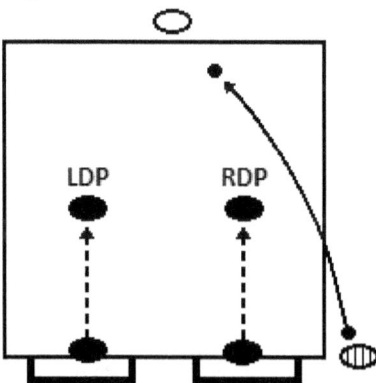

LDP    RDP

– while the attacking player performs a pass into the net defending players should move back moving backwards or half-sideways forward up to the moment when they define the direction of the ball;

– the attacking player should send the ball into the net with a mounted trajectory with a shot of medium power and not with a powerful shot with a linear trajectory;

Task 2 continuation

The attacking player receives the ball and sends it with a first touch without a delay with a mounted trajectory into one of goals with a medium speed from the outside of the playground.

When the attacking player begins to perform a pass, defending players begin to move back, moving backwards or half-sideways forward and trying to be approx. in parallel to each other at 7-8 meters (fig. 3).

– defending players should quickly define the direction of the ball sent into the net and knock it out, preventing from crossing the goal-line;

– to the moment when one of defending players knocks out the ball another should be 5-6 meters from him and on the same line across the width of the pitch or somewhat closer to the goal-line

**Fig. 3**

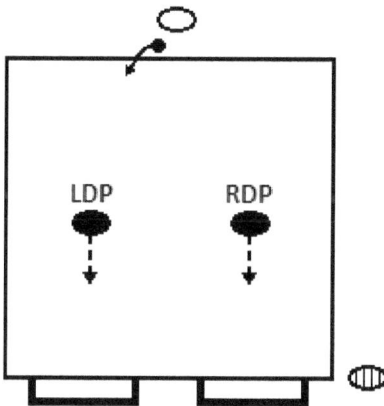

Having defined the direction of the ball, the defending player in whose goal the ball is sent moves to the goal and, having prevented the ball from crossing the goal-line, knocks it with a head or a foot through one of short sides of the playground or with a mounted trajectory towards the attacking player.

Task 2 continuation

Another defending player moves towards partner so that to be approx. 5-6 meters from him and on the same line across the width of the pitch or somewhat closer to the goal-line to the moment when the partner knocks the ball out (fig. 4).

**Fig. 4**

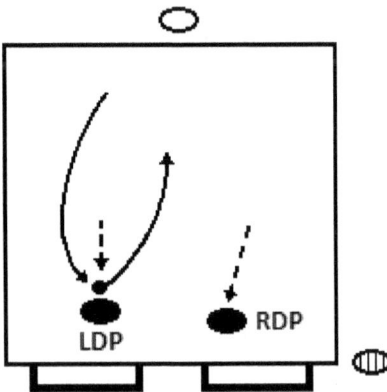

**Variants:**
a) defending players perform the task, having swapped their initial positions;
b) points of the attacking player's initial position across the width of the pitch are varied;
c) speed of performance of preparative actions for sending the ball into the bet by the attacking player (successive touches of the ball come one after another without a delay or with some delay between the first and the second touches and between the second and the third touches);

Task 2 continuation

| d) players' assistant and the attacking player are positioned in the initial position so that the former is able to perform passes to the attacking player on 15-20 meters at different angles across the width and along the length of the pitch from the left and from the right (fig. 5 and 6) | |
|---|---|

**Fig. 5**

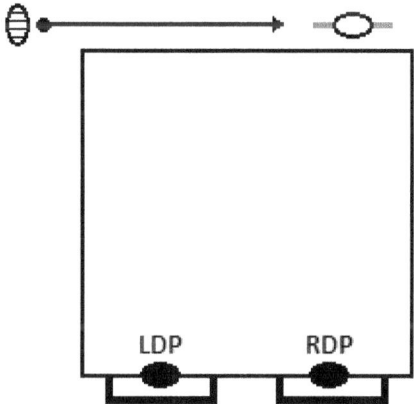

**Fig. 6**

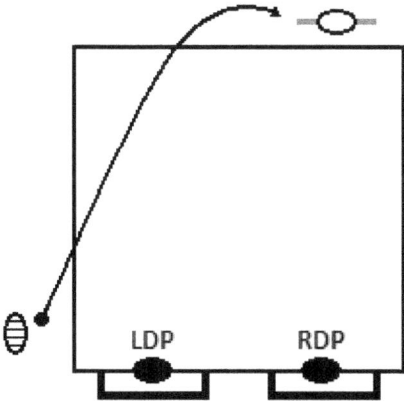

**Task 3. Pass back to the attacking player of a back line, two defending players' going forward when the ball is moving to this attacking player, two defending players' moving back and knocking the ball, sent by the attacking player of a back line into the area behind defending players' back, on a way of the attacking player of a front line who has left the offside, by one of them**

| Task description | Requirements for task performance quality |
|---|---|
| Playground 15 meters long and 16 meters wide is marked. Two attacking and two defending players are situated: <br> – the attacking player of a back line (APBL) – beyond the playground at its long side face to the playground; <br> – the attacking player of a front line (APFL) – at the middle of the opposite long side of the playground face to the partner; <br> – the right defending player (RDP) and the left defending player (LDP) – at that long side of the playground where the attacking player of a front line is situated, 4 meters from its ends and 8 meters from each other face to the attacking player of a back line. One of defending players has the ball (fig. 1). The defending player sends the ball to the attacking player of a back line with a foot over the pitch surface or with a mounted trajectory. Right after a pass the defending player begins quickly move towards the attacking player of a back line. | – right after the performance of a pass by one of defending players they should begin moving forward simultaneously and stop timely relative to the distance between the ball and the attacking player; <br> – while moving forward, defending players should try to be 7-8 meters from each other and on the same line across the width of the pitch; <br> – defending players should not begin to move back untimely, i.e. at the moment when the ball flying to the attacking player is still at sufficiently long distance from him; <br> – the attacking player of a front line should not delayed the beginning of leaving an offside; |

Task 3 continuation

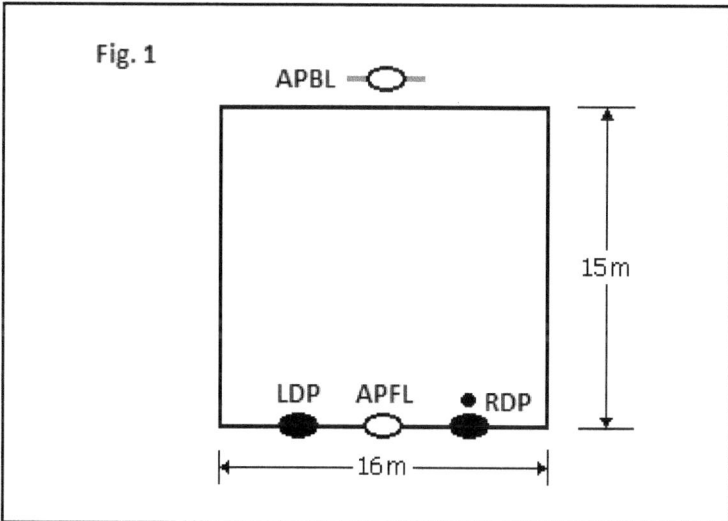

Fig. 1

While moving forward, defending players try to be approx. in parallel to each other at 7-8 meters. To the moment when the ball appears in close vicinity to the attacking player of a back line defending players stop moving forward. Right after defending players has begun going forward the attacking player begins to move quickly towards the position of the attacking player of a back line and leaves an offside (fig. 2). The attacking player of a back line receives the ball and gets ready to perform a pass.

Once the attacking player of a front line leaves an offside, defending players take such position that this player was in front of them.

The attacking player of a front line begins to move quickly to the area behind defending players' back for receiving the ball on a way.

– after the attacking player of a front line has left an offside defending players should quickly take such position that this player was in front of them;

– the attacking player of a front line should quickly move to the area behind defending players' back;

– the attacking player of a front line should vary the direction of movement into the area behind defending players' back;

## Task 3 continuation

**Fig. 2**

APBL ⊙

LDP  APFL  RDP

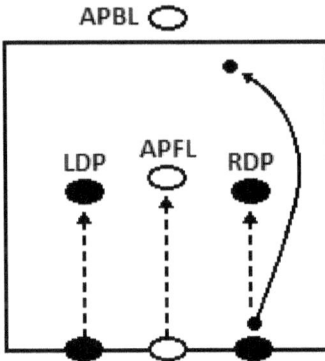

When the attacking player of a front line begins to open:
– defending players begin to move back, moving backwards or half-sideways forward and trying to be approx. in parallel to each other at 7-8 meters;
– the attacking player of a back line begins to perform a pass with a mounted trajectory with a medium speed from the outside of the playground so that the attacking player of a front line can touch it in the area behind defending players' back (fig. 3). Having defined the direction of sending the ball:
– the defending player, in whose zone of responsibility the ball is sent, moves to the ball and knocks it with a head or a foot without allowing the attacking player to touch the ball through one of short sides of the playground or with a mounted trajectory towards the attacking player of a back line;

– defending players should anticipate the moment of a pass by the attacking player of a back line into the area behind their back on his preparative actions to a pass performance and beginning of strike motion;
– while the attacking player of a back line performs a pass defending players should move back moving backwards or half-sideways forward up to the moment when they define the direction of the ball;
– defending players should quickly define the direction of the ball sent by the attacking player of a back line and knock it out, preventing the attacking player of a front line from touching the ball;
– to the moment when one of defending players knocks out the ball another should be 5-6 meters from him and on the same line across the width of the pitch or somewhat closer than him to the distant from the attacking player of a back line long side of the playground;

Task 3 continuation

Fig. 3

APBL

LDP    APFL    RDP

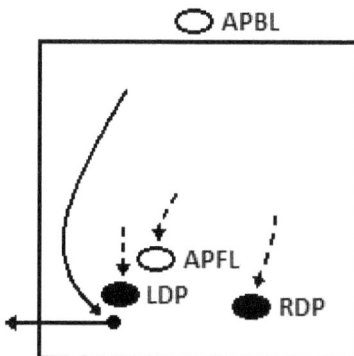

– the attacking player of a front line should move to the ball until the moment when the defending player knocks the ball out, but act not with a maximum activity

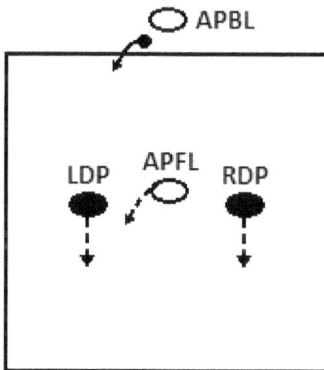

– the another defending player moves so that to be approx. 5 meters from the partner and somewhat closer than him to the distant from the attacking player of a back line long side of the playground at the moment when the ball is knocked out by the partner (fig. 4).

Fig. 4

APBL

APFL
LDP    RDP

Task 3 continuation

Offsides are given only until the moment when the attacking player of a front line leaves an offside.

**Variants:**

a) defending players perform the task, having swapped their initial positions;

b) directions in which the attacking player of a front line leaves an offside are varied;

c) points of attacking players' initial position across the width of the pitch are varied (fig. 5)

**Fig. 5**

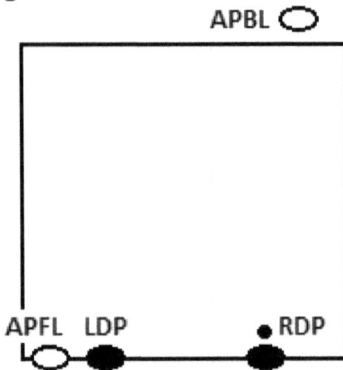

**Task 4. Pass back to one of two attacking players, two defending players' going forward when the ball is moving to the attacking player, two defending players' moving back and knocking out the ball, sent by one of attacking players into the area behind defending players' back, by one of them on a way of the another attacking player moving from the deep**

| Task description | Requirements for task performance quality |
|---|---|
| Playground 15 meters long and 16 meters wide is marked.<br>Two attacking and two defending players are situated:<br>– the right attacking player (RAP) and the left attacking player (LAP) – beyond the playground at its long side few meters from each other face to the playground;<br>– the right defending player (RDP) and the left defending player (LDP) – at the opposite long side of the playground 4 meters from its corners and 8 meters from each other face to attacking players.<br>One of attacking players has the ball (fig. 1).<br>The attacking player sends the ball towards defending players with a foot over the pitch surface or with a mounted trajectory.<br>One of defending players sends the ball with a foot with a first or a second fast performed touch or with a head to one of attacking players (fig. 2). | – right after the performance of a pass by one of defending players they should begin moving forward simultaneously and stop timely relative to the distance between the ball and the attacking player;<br>– while moving forward, defending players should try to be 7-8 meters from each other and on the same line across the width of the pitch;<br>– defending players should not begin to move back untimely, i.e. at the moment when the ball flying to the attacking player is still at sufficiently long distance from him;<br>– the attacking players with the ball and without it should act simultaneously; |

Task 4 continuation

Fig. 1

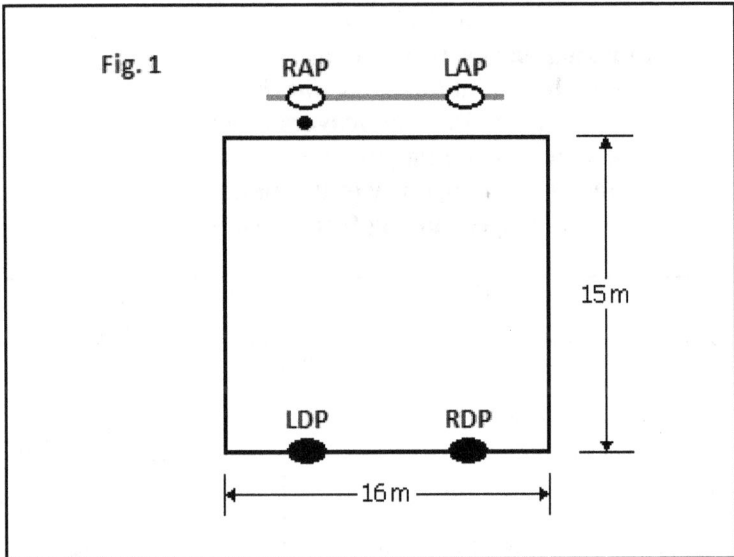

Fig. 2

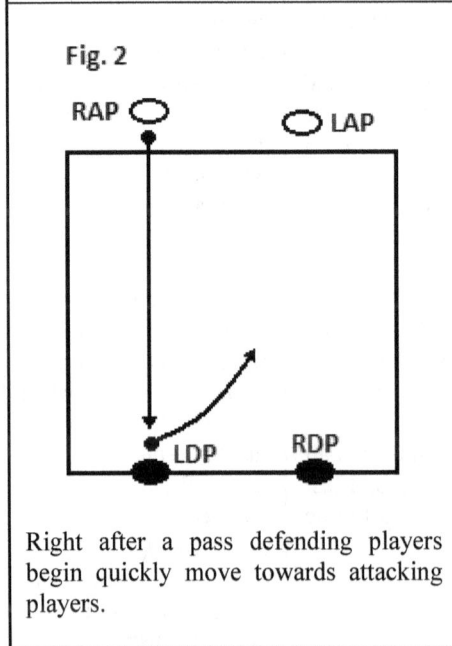

Right after a pass defending players begin quickly move towards attacking players.

– the attacking player should quickly move to the area behind defending players' back;– the attacking player without the ball should vary the direction of movement into the area behind defending players' back;

– defending players should anticipate the moment of a pass by the attacking player into the area behind their back on his preparative actions to a pass performance and beginning of strike motion;

Task 4 continuation

While moving forward, defending players try to be approx. in parallel to each other at 7-8 meters. To the moment when the ball appears in close vicinity to one of the attacking player defending players stop moving forward (fig. 3).

**Fig. 3**

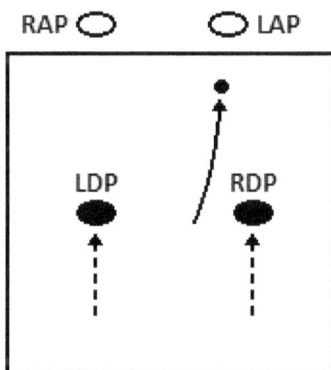

RAP ◯          ◯ LAP

LDP          RDP

The attacking player receives the ball sent to him and gets ready to perform a pass.

Once one of attacking players receives the ball, the another begins to move quickly to the area behind defending players' back, for receiving the ball on a way.

When the attacking player without the ball begins to open:

– defending players should respond timely to the beginning of movement of the attacking player for receiving the ball into the area behind their back;

– while the attacking player performs a pass defending players should move back moving backwards or half-sideways forward up to the moment when they define the direction of the ball;

– defending players should quickly define the direction of the ball sent by one of attacking players and knock it out, preventing another attacking player from touching the ball;

– to the moment when one of defending players knocks out the ball another should be 5-6 meters from him and on the same line across the width of the pitch or somewhat closer than him to the distant from the attacking player, who has performed a pass, long side of the playground;

Task 4 continuation

– defending players begin to move back, moving backwards or half-sideways forward and trying to be approx. in parallel to each other at 7-8 meters;
– the attacking player possessing the ball begins to perform a pass with a mounted trajectory with a medium speed from the outside of the playground so that the partner can touch it in the area behind defending players' back (fig. 4).

– the attacking player trying to receive the ball in the area behind defending players' back should move to the ball until the moment when the defending player knocks the ball out, but act not with a maximum activity

**Fig. 4**

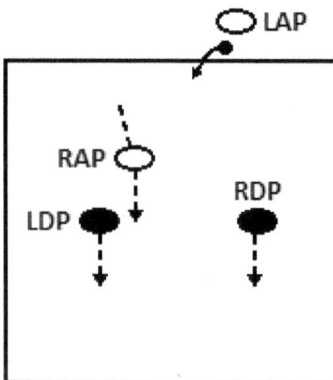

Having defined the direction of sending the ball:
– the defending player, in whose zone of responsibility the ball is sent, moves to the ball and knocks it with a head or a foot without allowing the attacking player to touch the ball through one of short sides of the playground or with a mounted trajectory towards the attacking player who performed a pass;

Task 4 continuation

– another defending player moves so that to be approx. 5 meters from the partner and somewhat closer than him to the distant from the attacking player, who has performed a pass, long side of the playground at the moment when the ball is knocked out by the partner (fig. 5);

**Fig. 5**

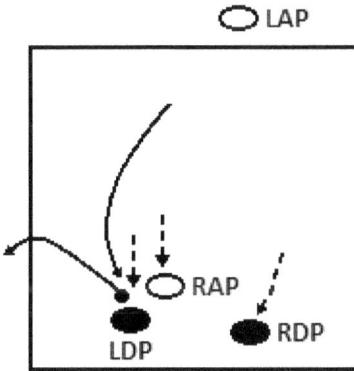

**Offsides are not given.**
**Variants:**
a) defending players perform the task, having swapped their initial positions;
b) points of attacking players' initial position across the width of the pitch and direction of their passes to the one of defending players are varied;
c) directions of movement of the attacking player without the ball into the area behind defending players' back

# CHAPTER 6.
## DEFENDING PLAYERS' LEARNING IN «TWO ON ATTACKING PLAYER MOVING WITH THE BALL TOWARDS THEM ALONG THE LENGTH OF THE PITCH» SITUATIONS

### 6. 1. Tasks and emphasis of the work

While learning the defensive play in «two on the attacking player without the ball moving with the ball towards them along the length of the pitch» it is necessary to learn footballers two main kinds of action.

**First.** To go at the attacking player moving with the ball in this defending player's zone of responsibility timely and tackle the ball or knock it out.

**Second.** To cover the partner who goes to knock or tackle the ball first.

In the course of learning these actions the attention is focused on development of players' abilities and skills of psychomotor character as follows:

– quickness of defining of the attacking player with the ball direction and speed of movement;

– proper performance of preparative actions before direct knocking or tackling the ball and actually knocking or tackling the ball;

– well-timed occupation of a necessary position while covering the partner.

With that the effective methodological technique is providing for defending players the uncertainty of point of beginning of the attacking player with the ball movement towards them and varying of his movement direction and speed.

# 6. 2. Drills for learning actions as a couple while moving of the attacking player with the ball in zone of responsibility of one of defending players all the time

**Task 1. Sudden pass to one of attacking players, quick move of the attacking player with the ball towards the defending player closer to him with a view to deliver the ball using dribbling into the area behind his back, tackling or knocking the ball out by this defending player and covering the partner by another defending player**

| Task description | Requirements for task performance quality |
|---|---|
| Two parallel lines 10 and 16 meters long are marked 12 meters from one another. Two attacking players, two defending players and the assistant are positioned: <br> – the right attacking player (RAP) and the left attacking player (LAP) – at the ends of boundary line 10 meters long face to boundary line 16 meters long; <br> – the right defending player (RDP) and the left defending player (LDP) – at the boundary line 16 meters long 4 meters from its ends and 8 meters from each other face to attacking players; <br> – players' assistant with the ball - at the middle of boundary line 10 meters long face to defending players (fig. 1). <br> The attacking players' assistant suddenly sends the ball at the one of the attacking players' foot. | – the attacking player to whom the ball was sent should begin moving quickly towards the defending player closest to him with a first touch of the ball and try to outplay him quickly; <br> – the defending player who meets the attacking player with the ball first should begin to get ready to tackle or knock the ball out timely; |

Task 1 continuation

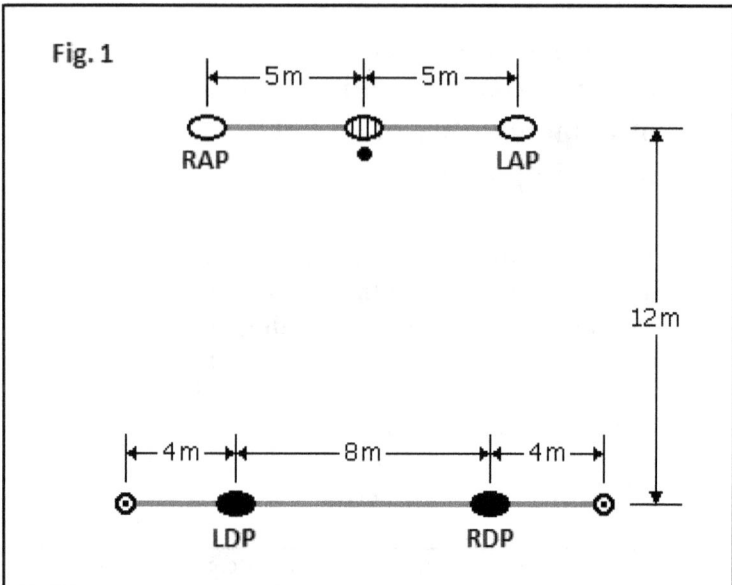

Fig. 1

The attacking player receives the ball, quickly move towards the defending player closest to him aiming to cross boundary line in the area behind this defending player's back (fig. 2).

The defending player at whom the attacking player with the ball moves slightly goes at the opponent to tackle or knock the ball out. While getting ready to tackle or knock out the ball and beginning to perform these actions he should:

– provoke the attacking player to move with the ball in the direction between defending players;

– to eliminate a possibility of attacking player with the ball going through boundary line from the side distant relative to another defending player.

– the defending player who meets the attacking player with the ball first should by no means give him a possibility to cross boundary line with the ball from the side distant relative to another defending player, and provoke him to move in direction between defending players;

Task 1 continuation

## Fig. 2

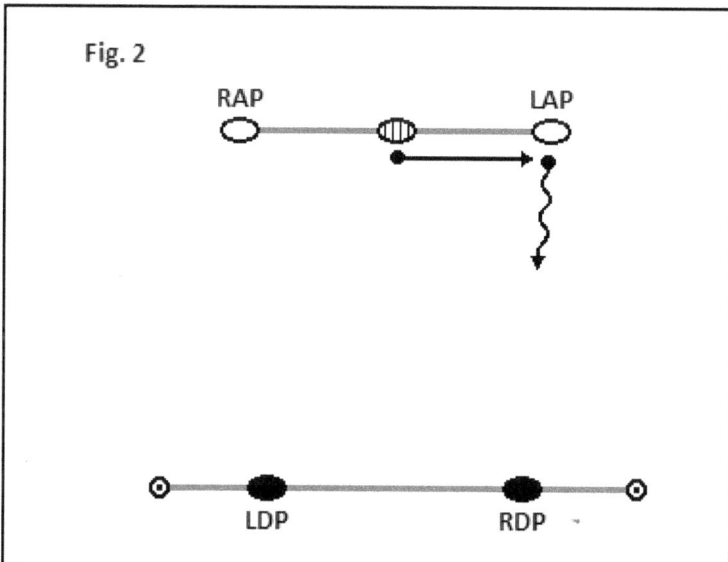

While the defending player, on whom the attacking player with the ball moves, gets ready to tackle or knock the ball out, the second one begins to move towards partner.

He moves in such a manner that to be diagonally to the partner to the moment when the attacking player begins to outplay defending player meeting him first: 3-4 meters across the width of the pitch and 1-2 meters further relative to the attacking player with the ball along the length of the pitch (fig. 3).

The defending player, on whom the attacking player moves, tries to tackle or knock the ball out from him.

If he fails to do so, then the ball should be tackled or knocked out by the second defending player, who tries to act depending on direction of the attacking player movement as following:

– the defending player who meets the attacking player with the ball should not be stiff-legged while performing preparative actions for tackling or knocking the ball out and directly while performing tackling or knocking the ball out;

– the defending player covering the partner should timely begin moving towards him;

Task 1 continuation

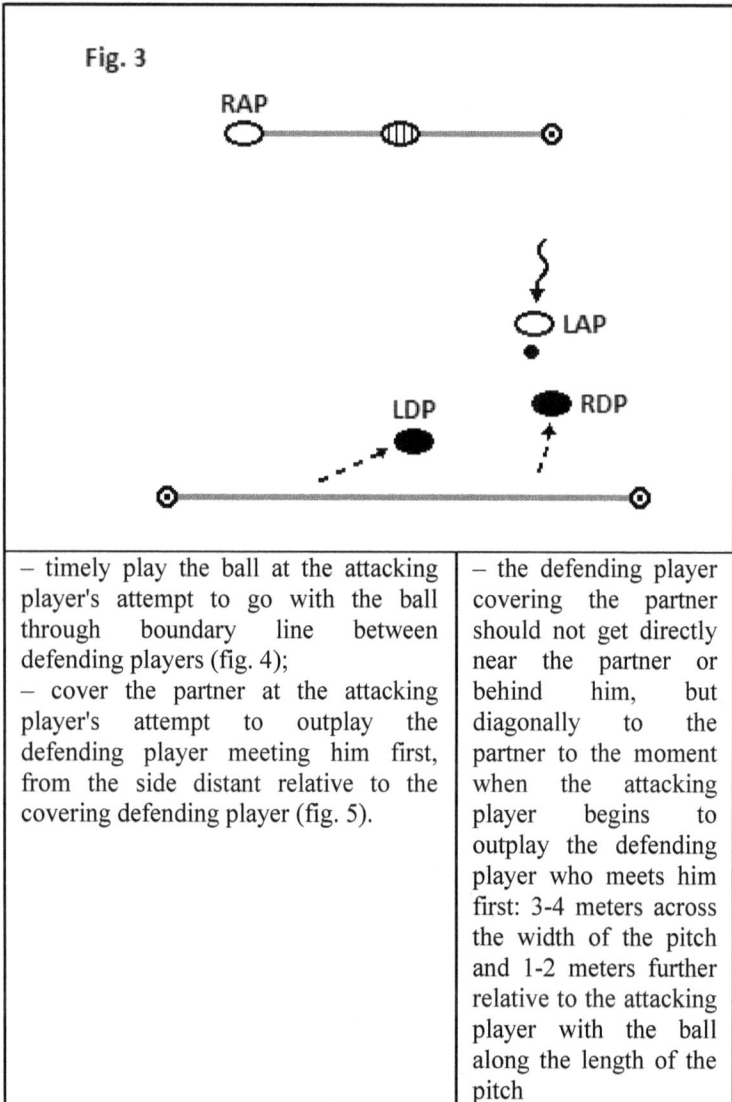

Fig. 3

RAP

LAP

LDP    RDP

– timely play the ball at the attacking player's attempt to go with the ball through boundary line between defending players (fig. 4);
– cover the partner at the attacking player's attempt to outplay the defending player meeting him first, from the side distant relative to the covering defending player (fig. 5).

– the defending player covering the partner should not get directly near the partner or behind him, but diagonally to the partner to the moment when the attacking player begins to outplay the defending player who meets him first: 3-4 meters across the width of the pitch and 1-2 meters further relative to the attacking player with the ball along the length of the pitch

Task 1 continuation

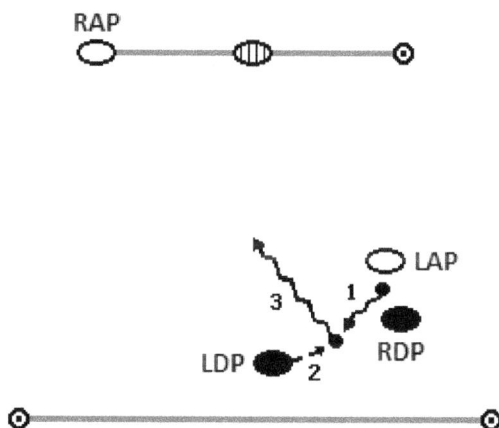

Fig. 4

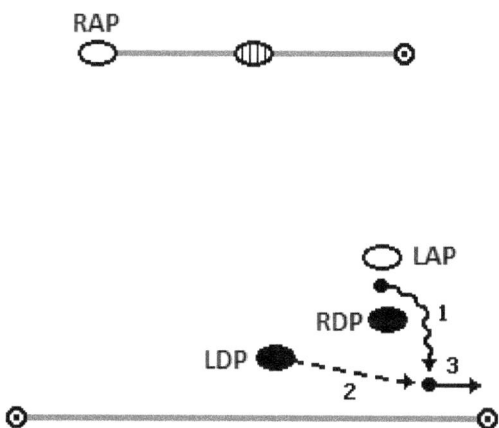

Fig. 5

| **Variant:** defending players perform the task, having swapped their initial positions | |

**Task 2. Sudden pass to one of attacking players, quick move of the attacking player with the ball towards the defending player closer to him with a view to deliver the ball using a pass or outplaying into the area behind his back, quick going of this defending player forward, interception, tackling or knocking the ball out by him and covering the partner by another defending player**

| Task description | Requirements for task performance quality |
|---|---|
| Two parallel lines 10 and 16 meters long are marked 15 meters from one another.<br>Two goal 5 meters wide marked with cones are mounted on boundary line 16 meters long at its ends.<br>Two attacking players, two defending players and the assistant are positioned:<br>– the right attacking player (RAP) and the left attacking player (LAP) – at the ends of boundary line 10 meters long face to boundary line 16 meters long;<br>– the right defending player (RDP) and the left defending player (LDP) – at the boundary line 16 meters long 4 meters from its ends and 8 meters from each other face to attacking players;<br>– players' assistant with the ball – at the middle of boundary line 10 meters long face to defending players (fig. 1).<br>The attacking players' assistant suddenly sends the ball at the one of the attacking players' foot.<br>The attacking player receives the ball, quickly moves towards the defending player closest to him aiming to: | – the attacking player to whom the ball was sent should begin moving quickly towards the defending player closest to him with a first touch of the ball and try to outplay him quickly or send the ball into the net;<br>– the defending player who meets the attacking player with the ball first should move on him timely and quickly and try to begin intercepting, tackling or knocking the ball out from the attacking player at the maximum possible distance from boundary line 16 meters long; |

Task 2 continuation

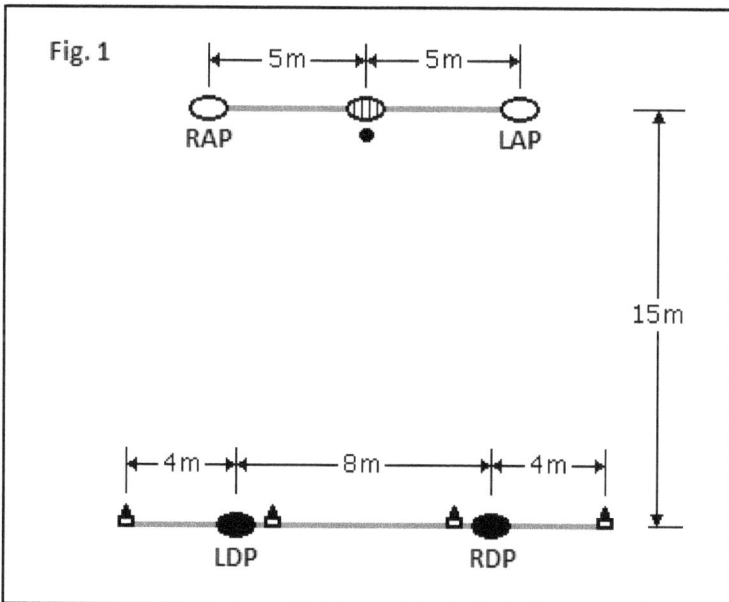

Fig. 1

- send the ball over the pitch surface beyond boundary line through the goal behind this defending player's back;
- cross boundary line with the ball in the area behind this defending player's back (fig. 2).

The defending player at whom the attacking player with the ball moves quickly goes as close to the opponent as possible to tackle or knock the ball out from him. While getting ready to tackle or knock out the ball and beginning to perform these actions he should:
- to preclude the attacking player from sending the ball into the net behind the back, firstly from the side distant relative to another defending player;
- provoke the attacking player to move with the ball in the direction between defending players;

- the defending player who meets the attacking player with the ball first should by no means give him a possibility to send the ball into the net from the side distant relative to another defending player, and try to intercept the ball in case the attacking player sends it into the net between defending players;

Task 2 continuation

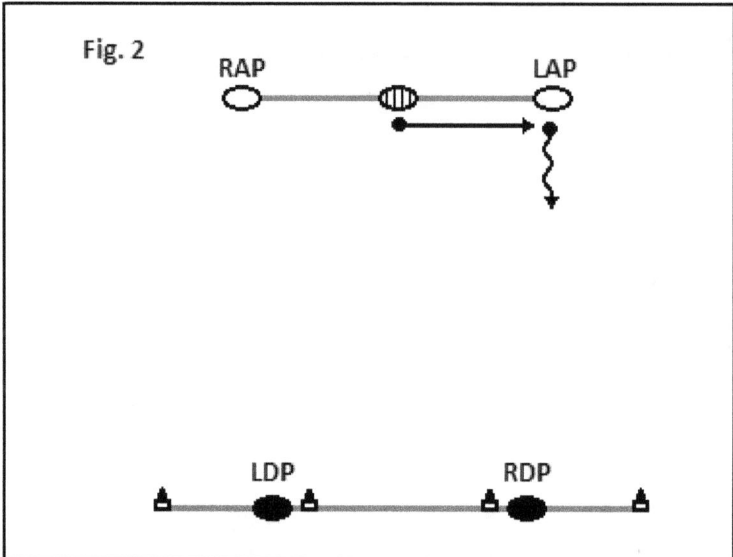

Fig. 2

- to eliminate a possibility of attacking player with the ball going through boundary line from the side distant relative to another defending player. While the defending player, on whom the attacking player with the ball moves, gets ready to tackle or knock the ball out, the second one begins to move towards partner. He moves in such a manner that to be diagonally to the partner to the moment when the attacking player begins to send the ball into the net or to outplay defending player meeting him first:
- at 4-5 meters across the width of the pitch when the attacking player sends the ball into the net;
- 3-4 meters across the width of the pitch and 1-2 meters further relative to the attacking player with the ball along the length of the pitch when he performs outplaying (fig. 3).

- the defending player who meets the attacking player with the ball first should by no means give him a possibility to cross boundary line with the ball from the side distant relative to another defending player, and provoke him to move in direction between defending players;

Task 2 continuation

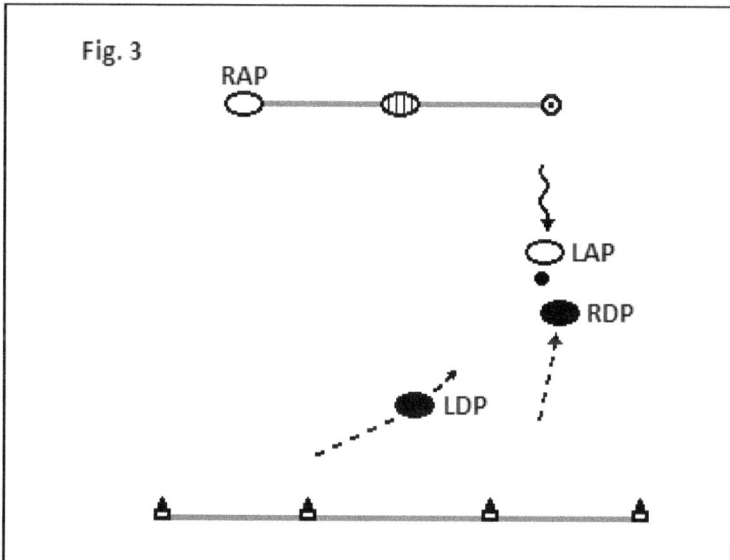

Fig. 3

The defending player meeting the attacking player tries to intercept the ball, if the attacking player sends it into the net, or tackle or knock it out, if the attacking player tries to cross boundary line with the ball.

If he fails to do so, then the ball should be intercepted, tackled or knocked out by the second defending player, who tries to act depending on variant of actions direction of the attacking player movement as following:

– get in time to intercept the ball if the attacking players sends it into the net between defending players (fig. 4);

– timely play the ball at the attacking player's attempt to go with the ball through boundary line between defending players (fig. 5);

– the defending player who meets the attacking player with the ball should not be stiff-legged while performing preparative actions for tackling or knocking the ball out and directly while performing tackling or knocking the ball out;

– the defending player covering the partner should timely begin moving towards him;

## Task 2 continuation

| | |
|---|---|
| – cover the partner at the attacking player's attempt to outplay the defending player meeting him first, from the side distant relative to the covering defending player (fig. 6). | – the defending player covering the partner should not get directly near the partner or behind him, but diagonally to the partner to the moment when the attacking player begins to outplay the defending player who meets him first: 3-4 meters across the width of the pitch and 1-2 meters further relative to the attacking player with the ball along the length of the pitch |

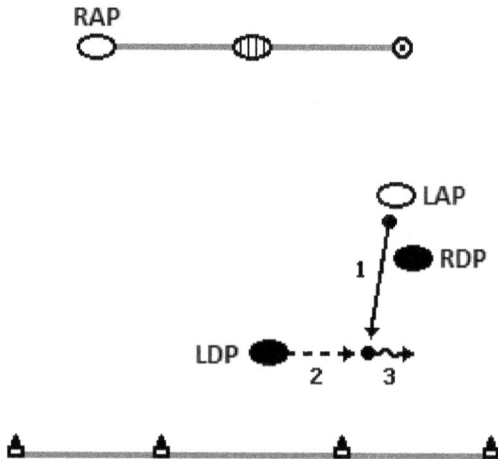

Fig. 4

Task 2 continuation

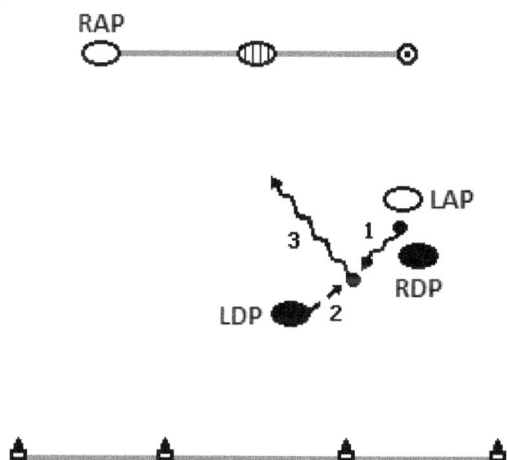

Fig. 5

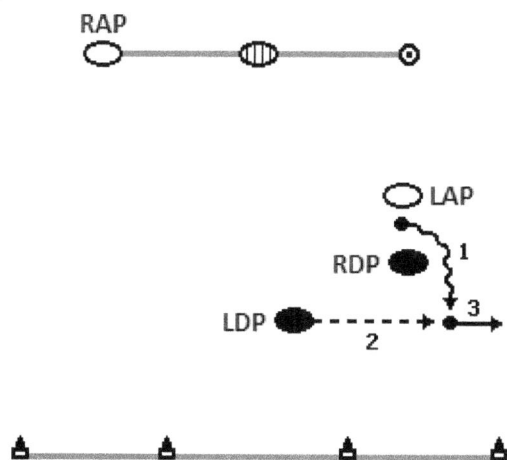

Fig. 6

| **Variant:** defending players perform the task, having swapped their initial positions | |
|---|---|

# 6. 3. Drills for learning actions as a couple while moving of the attacking player with the ball from one defending player's zone of responsibility to another

**Task 1. Sudden quick movement of one of attacking players with the ball towards defending players without or with moving from the one defending player's zone of responsibility to another with a view to deliver the ball using dribbling into the area behind their back, tackling or knocking the ball out by the one defending player and covering the partner by another defending player**

| Task description | Requirements for task performance quality |
| --- | --- |
| Two parallel lines 8 and 16 meters long are marked 15 meters from one another. Two attacking and two defending players are situated:<br>– the right attacking player (RAP) and the left attacking player (LAP) with balls – at the ends of boundary line 8 meters long face to boundary line 16 meters long;<br>– the right defending player (RDP) and the left defending player (LDP) – at the boundary line 16 meters long 4 meters from its ends and 8 meters from each other face to attacking players (fig. 1).<br>Suddenly one of attacking players begins to move with the ball quickly towards boundary line 16 meters long aiming to cross it. | – the attacking player should move with the ball quickly towards defending players and try to outplay them quickly;<br>– the attacking player should suddenly move with the ball from the one defending player's zone of responsibility to another;<br>– defending player should quickly define which of them would meet the attacking player with the ball first, and which would cover the partner; |

Task 1 continuation

**Fig. 1**

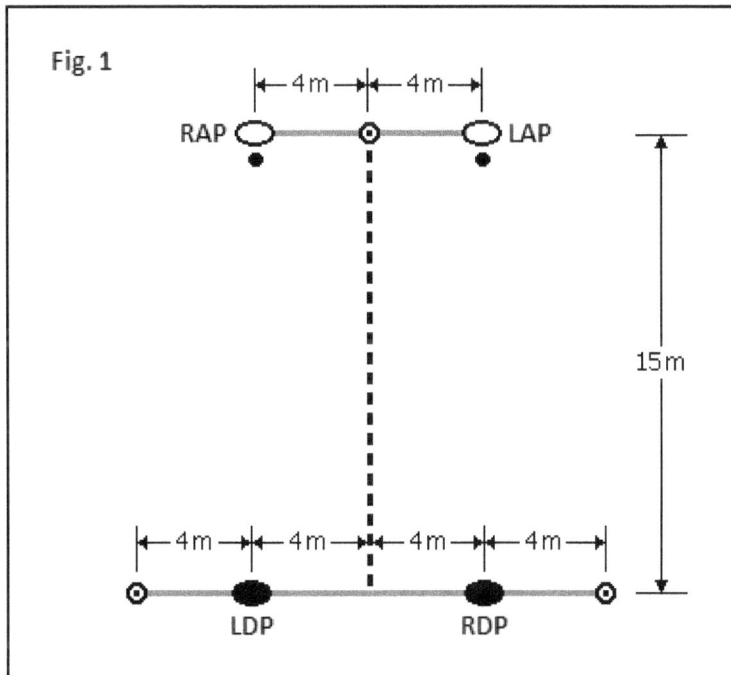

At different attempts the attacking player may move:
– towards the defending player closest to him all the time;
– towards the defending player closest to him at first, then towards the defending player distant to him (fig. 2). Slightly moving forward, defending players quickly identify the direction of the attacking player's movement and act as following.
The defending player, in whose zone of responsibility the attacking player is moving all the time or in whose zone of responsibility the attacking player has moved, goes at the opponent for tackling or knocking the ball out from him.

– the defending player who meets the attacking player with the ball first should begin to get ready to tackle or knock the ball out timely;
– the defending player who meets the attacking player with the ball first should by no means give him a possibility to cross boundary line with the ball from the side distant relative to another defending player, and provoke him to move in direction between defending players;

Task 1 continuation

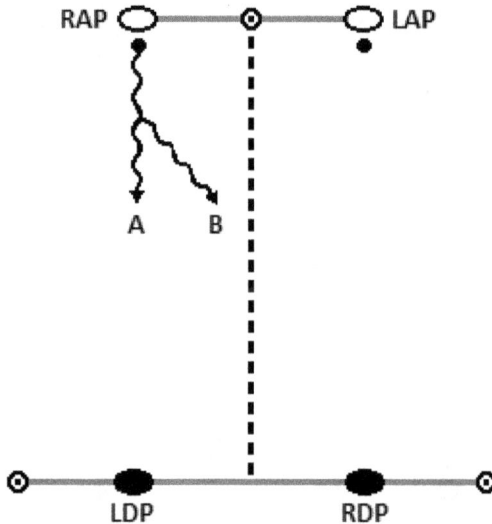

Fig. 2

While getting ready to tackle or knock out the ball and beginning to perform these actions he should:

– provoke the attacking player to move with the ball in the direction between defending players;

– to eliminate a possibility of attacking player with the ball going through boundary line from the side distant relative to another defending player.

While the defending player meeting the attacking player with the ball first, gets ready to tackle or knock the ball out, the another one begins to move towards partner.

– the defending player who meets the attacking player with the ball should not be stiff-legged while performing preparative actions for tackling or knocking the ball out and directly while performing tackling or knocking the ball out;

– the defending player covering the partner should timely begin moving towards him;

Task 1 continuation

He moves in such a manner that to be diagonally to the partner to the moment when the attacking player begins to outplay defending player meeting him first: 3-4 meters across the width of the pitch and 1-2 meters further relative to the attacking player with the ball along the length of the pitch (fig. 3 and 4).

The defending player, on whom the attacking player moves, tries to tackle or knock the ball out from him.

If he fails to do so, then the ball should be tackled or knocked out by the second defending player, who tries to act depending on direction of the attacking player movement as following:

– the defending player covering the partner should not get directly near the partner or behind him, but diagonally to the partner to the moment when the attacking player begins to outplay the defending player who meets him first: 3-4 meters across the width of the pitch and 1-2 meters further relative to the attacking player with the ball along the length of the pitch

**Fig. 3**

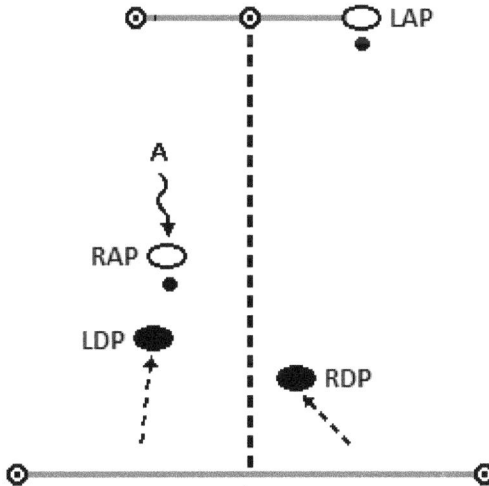

Task 1 continuation

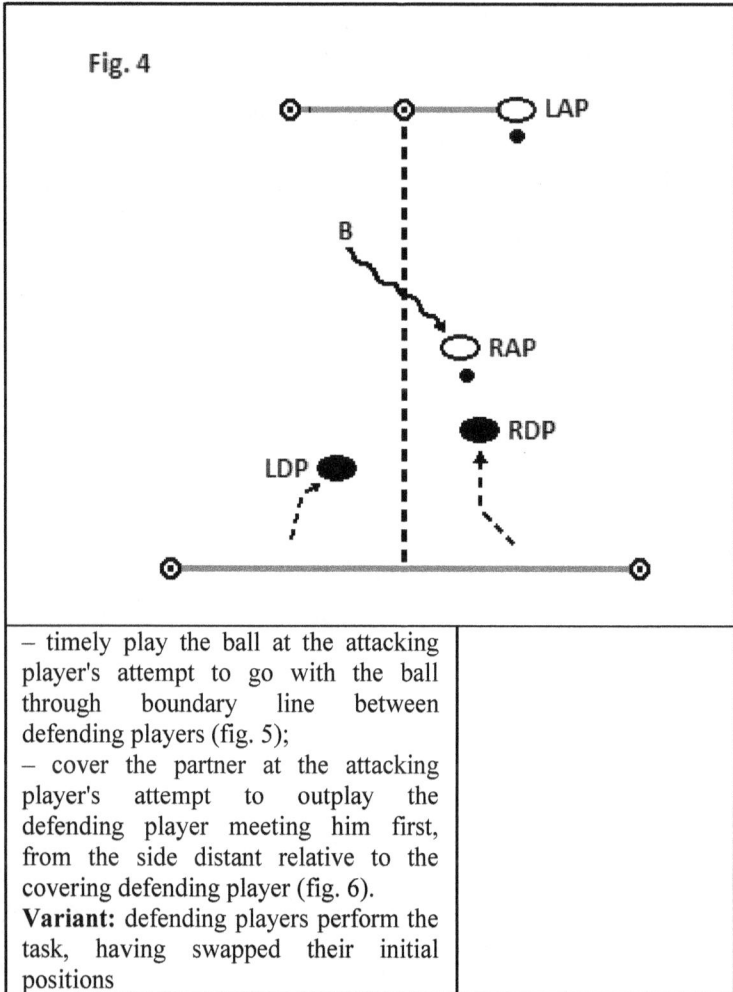

Fig. 4

− timely play the ball at the attacking player's attempt to go with the ball through boundary line between defending players (fig. 5);
− cover the partner at the attacking player's attempt to outplay the defending player meeting him first, from the side distant relative to the covering defending player (fig. 6).
**Variant:** defending players perform the task, having swapped their initial positions

Task 1 continuation

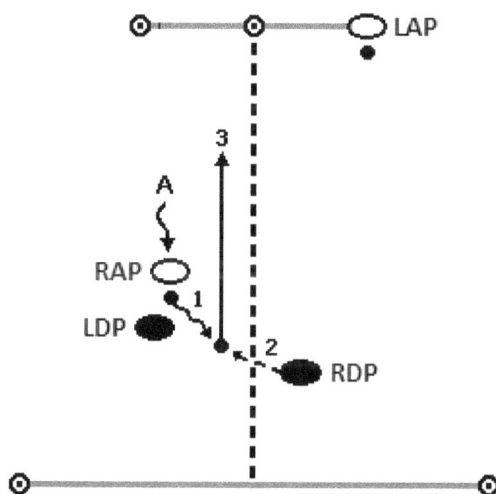

Fig. 5

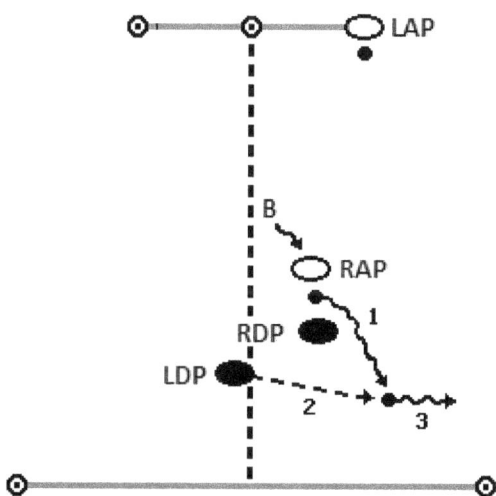

Fig. 6

**Task 2. Sudden quick movement of one of attacking players with the ball towards defending players without or with going from one defending player's zone of responsibility to another with a view to deliver the ball using a pass or dribbling into the area behind their back, quick going forward of one of defending players, interception, tackling or knocking the ball out by him and covering the partner by another defending player**

| Task description | Requirements for task performance quality |
|---|---|
| Two parallel lines 8 and 16 meters long are marked 15 meters from one another. Two goal 5 meters wide marked with cones are mounted on boundary line 16 meters long at its ends. Two attacking and two defending players are situated: <br> – the right attacking player (RAP) and the left attacking player (LAP) with balls – at the ends of boundary line 8 meters long face to boundary line 16 meters long; <br> – the right defending player (RDP) and the left defending player (LDP) – at the boundary line 16 meters long 4 meters from its ends and 8 meters from each other face to attacking players (fig. 1). <br> Suddenly one of attacking players begins to move with the ball quickly towards boundary line 16 meters long with a view to: <br> – send the ball over the pitch surface beyond boundary line through the goal behind one or another defending player's back; | – the attacking player moving with the ball quickly towards defending players and trying to outplay them quickly or send the ball into the net; <br> – the attacking player should suddenly move with the ball from the one defending player's zone of responsibility to another; <br> – defending player should quickly define which of them would meet the attacking player with the ball first, and which would cover the partner; |

Task 2 continuation

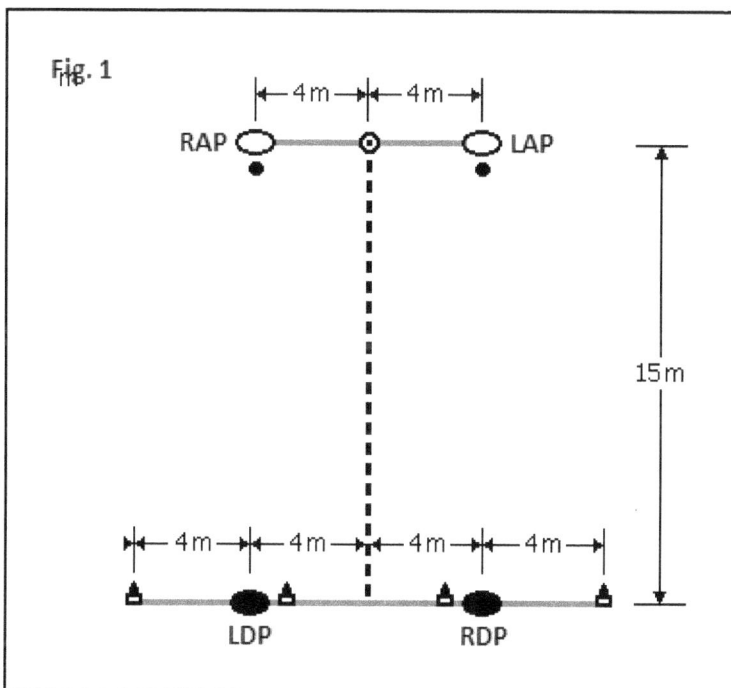

Fig. 1

<table>
<tr><td>

– cross boundary line with the ball in the area behind defending players' back. At different attempts the attacking player may move:

– towards the defending player closest to him all the time;

– towards the defending player closest to him at first, then towards the defending player distant to him (fig. 2). Slightly moving forward, defending players quickly identify the direction of the attacking player's movement and act as following.

</td><td>

– the defending player who meets the attacking player with the ball first should move on him timely and quickly and try to begin intercepting, tackling or knocking the ball out from the attacking player at the maximum possible distance from boundary line 16 meters long;

</td></tr>
</table>

Task 2 continuation

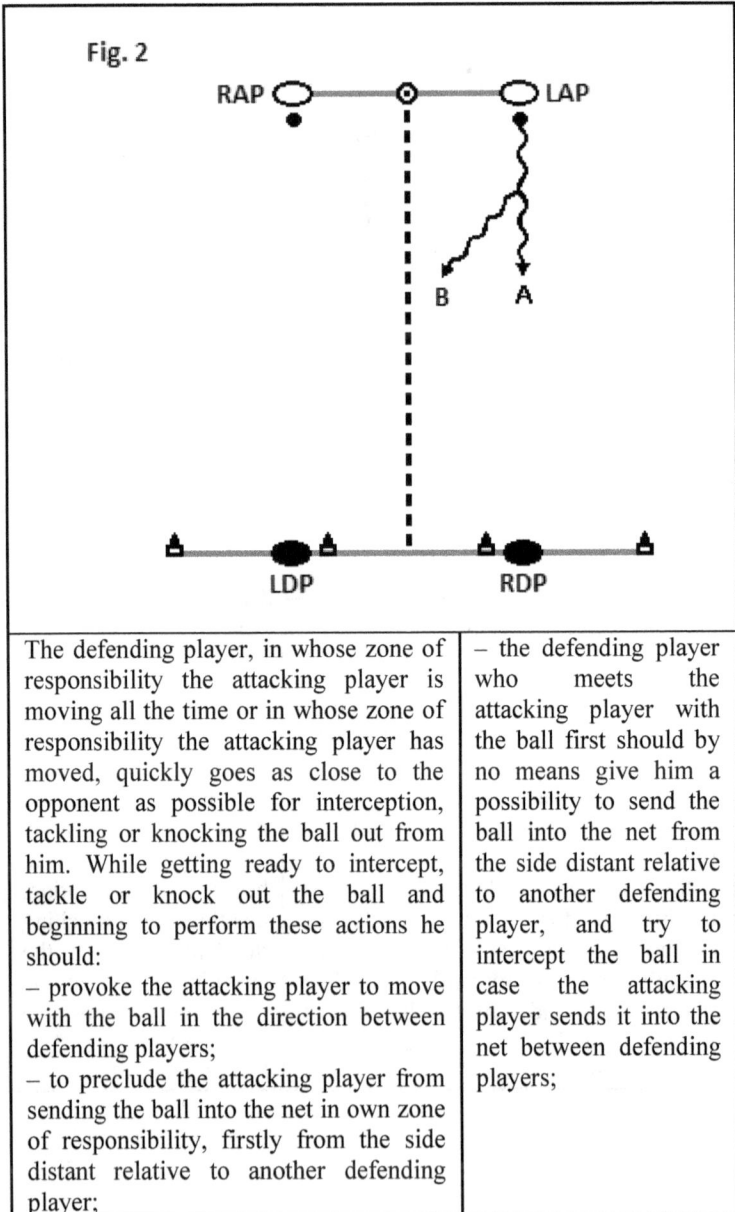

Fig. 2

The defending player, in whose zone of responsibility the attacking player is moving all the time or in whose zone of responsibility the attacking player has moved, quickly goes as close to the opponent as possible for interception, tackling or knocking the ball out from him. While getting ready to intercept, tackle or knock out the ball and beginning to perform these actions he should:
– provoke the attacking player to move with the ball in the direction between defending players;
– to preclude the attacking player from sending the ball into the net in own zone of responsibility, firstly from the side distant relative to another defending player;

– the defending player who meets the attacking player with the ball first should by no means give him a possibility to send the ball into the net from the side distant relative to another defending player, and try to intercept the ball in case the attacking player sends it into the net between defending players;

Task 2 continuation

– to eliminate a possibility of attacking player with the ball going through boundary line from the side distant relative to another defending player.

While the defending player meeting the attacking player with the ball first, gets ready to intercept, tackle or knock the ball out, the another one begins to move towards partner.

He moves in such a manner that to be diagonally to the partner to the moment when the attacking player begins to send the ball into the net or to outplay defending player meeting him first:

– at 4-5 meters across the width of the pitch when the attacking player sends the ball into the net;

– 3-4 meters across the width of the pitch and 1-2 meters further relative to the attacking player with the ball along the length of the pitch when he performs outplaying (fig. 3 and 4).

The defending player meeting the attacking player tries to intercept the ball, if the attacking player sends it into the net, or tackle or knock it out, if the attacking player tries to cross boundary line with the ball.

If he fails to do so, then the ball should be intercepted, tackled or knocked out by the second defending player, who tries to act depending on variant of actions direction of the attacking player movement as following:

– get in time to intercept the ball if the attacking players sends it into the net between defending players (fig. 5);

– the defending player who meets the attacking player with the ball first should by no means give him a possibility to cross boundary line with the ball from the side distant relative to another defending player, and provoke him to move in direction between defending players;

– the defending player who meets the attacking player with the ball should not be stiff-legged while performing preparative actions for tackling or knocking the ball out and directly while performing tackling or knocking the ball out;

– the defending player covering the partner should timely begin moving towards him;

## Task 2 continuation

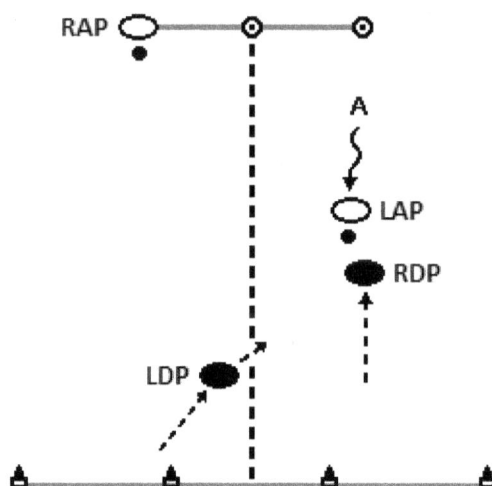

Fig. 3

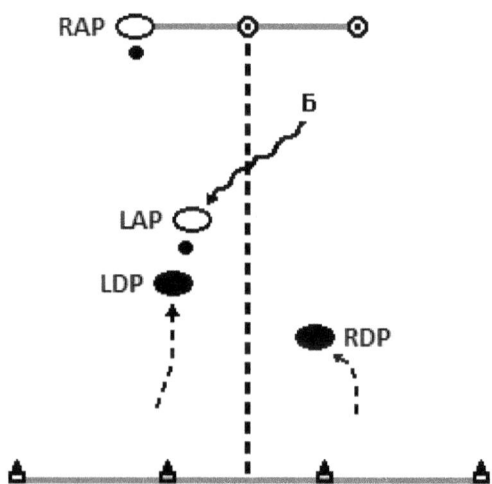

Fig. 4

Task 2 continuation

**Fig. 5**

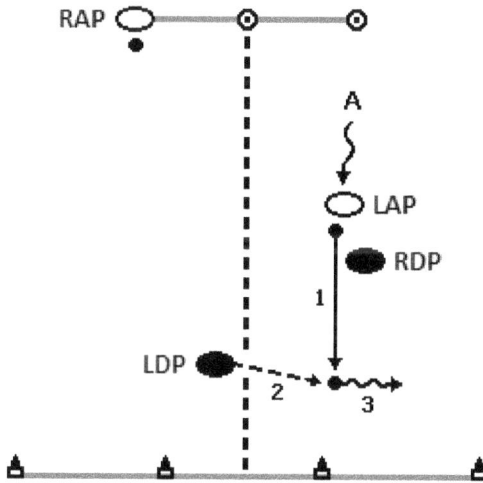

| | |
|---|---|
| – timely play the ball at the attacking player's attempt to go with the ball through boundary line between defending players (fig. 6); <br> – cover the partner at the attacking player's attempt to outplay the defending player meeting him first, from the side distant relative to the covering defending player (fig. 7). | – the defending player covering the partner should not get directly near the partner or behind him, but diagonally to the partner to the moment when the attacking player begins to outplay the defending player who meets him first: 3-4 meters across the width of the pitch and 1-2 meters further relative to the attacking player with the ball along the length of the pitch |

Task 2 continuation

Fig. 6

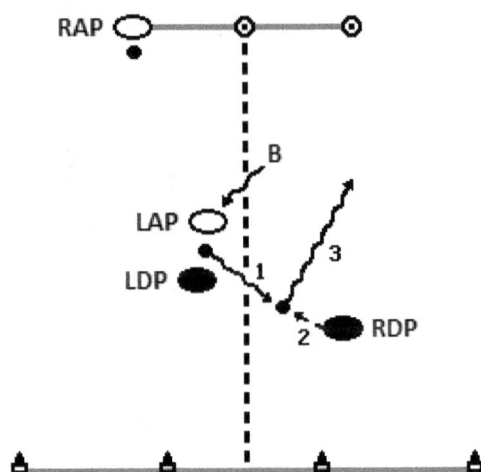

Fig. 7

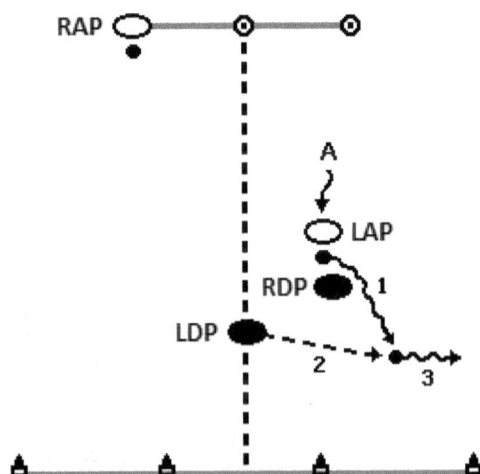

| Variant: defending players perform the task, having swapped their initial positions | |
|---|---|

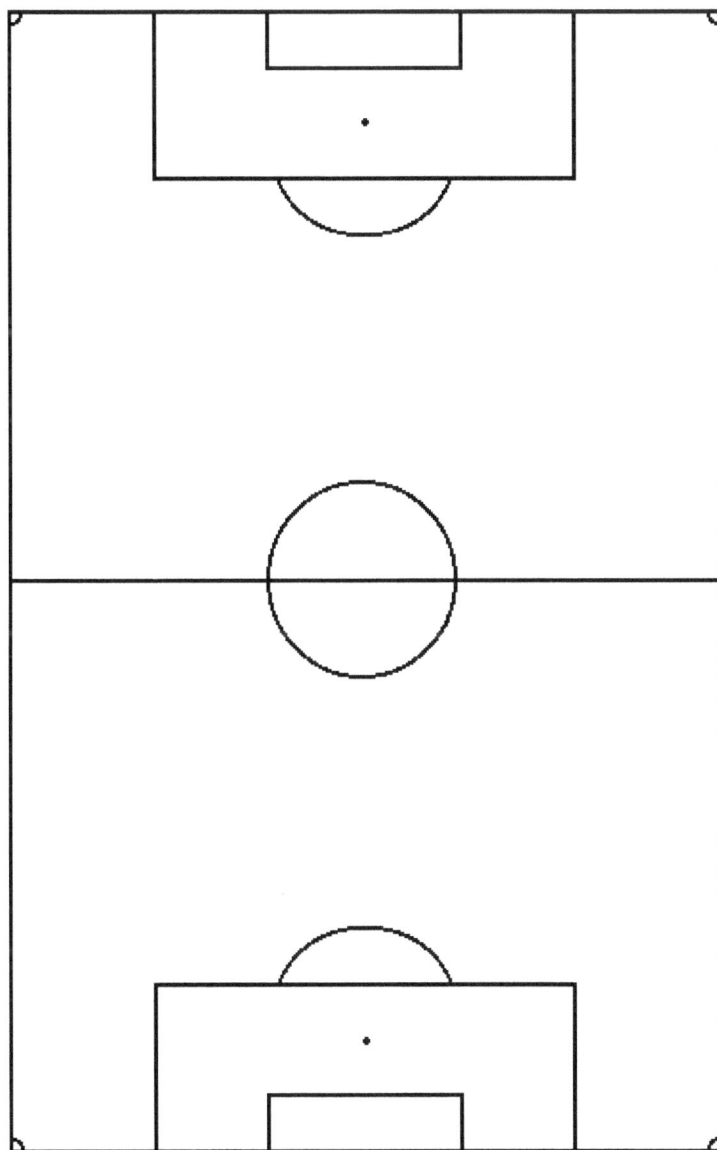

# For notes

# CHAPTER 7.
# DEFENDING PLAYERS' LEARNING OF ACTIONS IN «TWO ON ATTACKING PLAYER WITHOUT THE BALL SITUATED BETWEEN OF THEM ALONG THE LENGTH OF THE PITCH» SITUATIONS

## 7. 1. Tasks and emphasis of the work

While learning the defensive play in «two on the attacking player without the ball situated between them along the length of the pitch» it is necessary to learn footballers two main kinds of actions.

**First.** Squeeze the attacking player in a vise while restraint of his attempts to come over the ball after a pass at his foot.

**Second.** To keep a compact arrangement along the length of the pitch while restraint of the attacking player's attempts to come over the ball after a pass on his way.

In the course of learning these actions the attention is focused on development of players' abilities and skills of psychomotor character as follows:

– anticipation of a moment and direction of sending the ball to a marked player basing on actions of his partner performing a pass;

– speed of assessment of the ball trajectory;

– speed of movements to the ball sent at the opponent's foot or on his way.

With that the effective methodological technique is varying of distance and direction of passes to the attacking player and distance between defending players in initial position (from 8-10 to 13-15 meters).

# 7. 2. Drills for learning actions while passing the ball at the attacking player's foot

**Task 1. Moving back after performing a lengthwise pass by the attacking player and squeezing in a vise the attacking player, to whom the ball was sent, with another defending player**

| Task description | Requirements for task performance quality |
|---|---|
| Playground 20 meters long and 10 meters wide is marked, divided into four zones:<br>– the first – 3 meters long;<br>– the second – 10 meters long;<br>– the third – 3 meters long;<br>– the fourth – 4 meters long;<br>Two attacking and two defending players are situated:<br>– the attacking player of a front line (APFL) – at the line between the second and the third zones of the pitch face to the first zone;<br>– the attacking player of a back line (APBL) – at the short side of the playground beyond the first zone face to the playground;<br>– the defending player of a front line (DPFL) – at the line between the first and the second zones of the pitch face to the attacking player of a back line;<br>– the defending player of a back line (DPBL) – at the line between the third and the fourth zones of the pitch face to the attacking player of a front line (fig. 1). | – while getting ready to receive the ball from the partner, the attacking player of a front line should not enter the second zone of the pitch until the moment of performing a pass to him;<br>– while controlling actions of the attacking player of a front line, the defending player should not enter the third zone of the pitch until the moment of performing a pass to this player and should see actions of the attacking player possessing the ball with that;<br>– the attacking players with the ball and without it should act simultaneously; |

Task 1 continuation

Fig. 1

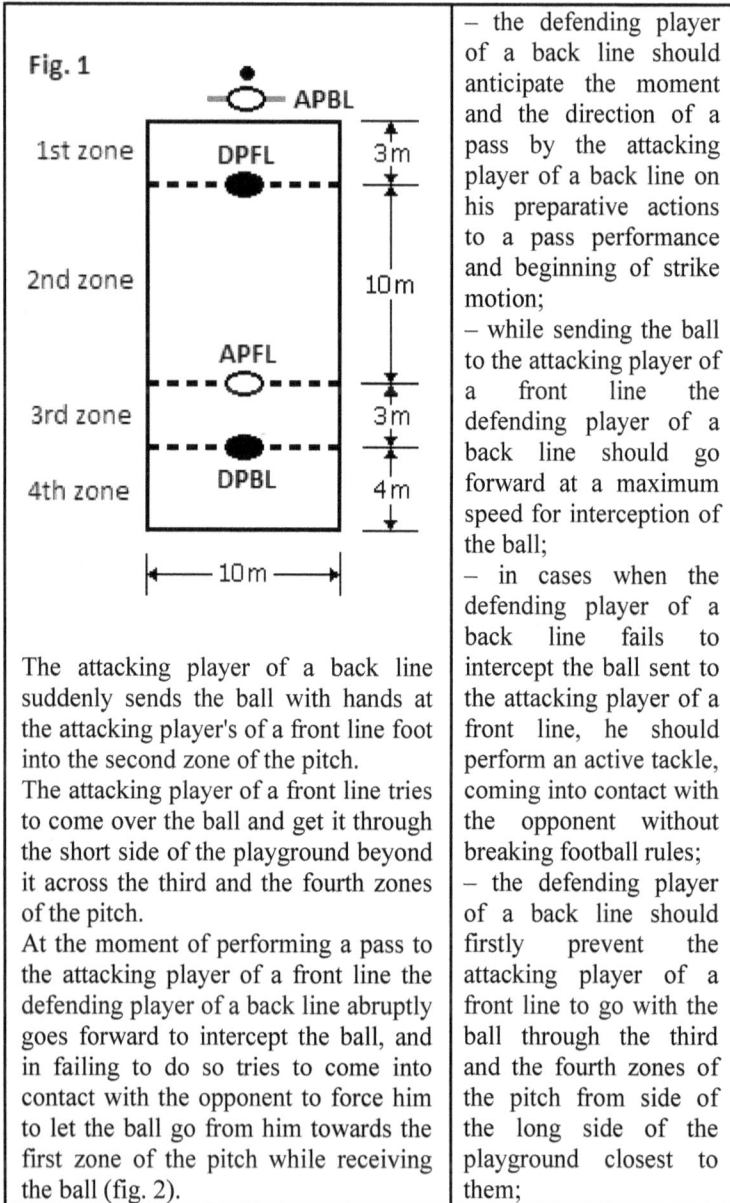

1st zone

2nd zone

3rd zone

4th zone

10 m

The attacking player of a back line suddenly sends the ball with hands at the attacking player's of a front line foot into the second zone of the pitch.

The attacking player of a front line tries to come over the ball and get it through the short side of the playground beyond it across the third and fourth zones of the pitch.

At the moment of performing a pass to the attacking player of a front line the defending player of a back line abruptly goes forward to intercept the ball, and in failing to do so tries to come into contact with the opponent to force him to let the ball go from him towards the first zone of the pitch while receiving the ball (fig. 2).

– the defending player of a back line should anticipate the moment and the direction of a pass by the attacking player of a back line on his preparative actions to a pass performance and beginning of strike motion;

– while sending the ball to the attacking player of a front line the defending player of a back line should go forward at a maximum speed for interception of the ball;

– in cases when the defending player of a back line fails to intercept the ball sent to the attacking player of a front line, he should perform an active tackle, coming into contact with the opponent without breaking football rules;

– the defending player of a back line should firstly prevent the attacking player of a front line to go with the ball through the third and the fourth zones of the pitch from side of the long side of the playground closest to them;

Task 1 continuation

| | |
|---|---|
| **Fig. 2** 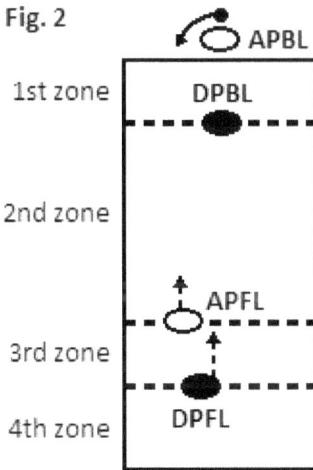 1st zone  DPBL  2nd zone  APFL  3rd zone  DPFL  4th zone | – the defending player of a back line should attack the attacking player of a front line in such a manner that the latter lets it go from himself; <br>– after the ball crosses the line of the defending player's position along the length of the pitch, he should turn face to the attacking player of a front line at once and quickly goes directly at him to come over the ball, but not into the area behind the defending player's of a back line back for covering the partner; <br>– when the attacking player of a front line receives the ball, the defending player of a front line should be at such distance from the opponent that the latter haven't got the space for actions with the ball; |

After the ball would cross the line of the defending player's of a front line position along the length of the pitch, he turns face to the attacking player of a front line at once and quickly goes directly at him (fig. 3).

As a result of such actions defending players should squeeze the attacking player of a front line in a vise and come over the ball (fig. 4).

If one of defending players come over the ball, he tries to get it to the first zone of the pitch (fig. 5 and 6).

The attacking player of a front line tries to prevent the defending player from getting the ball to the first zone of the pitch, not acting with a maximum activity.

If defending players intercept the ball sent to the attacking player of a front line or tackle the ball from him, then they gain 1 point.

Task 1 continuation

| | |
|---|---|
| If the attacking player gets the ball through the short side of the playground beyond it through the fourth zone of the pitch, he gains 5 points. | – the attacking player of a front line should try to receive the ball, including with the drifting, without letting it go far from him, and quickly move with the ball through the third and the fourth zones of the pitch; <br> – the defending player who has come over the ball should get it to the first zone of the pitch at a maximum speed; <br> – the attacking player of a front line trying to prevent the defending player from getting the ball to the first zone of the pitch, should not act with a maximum activity |

**Fig. 3**

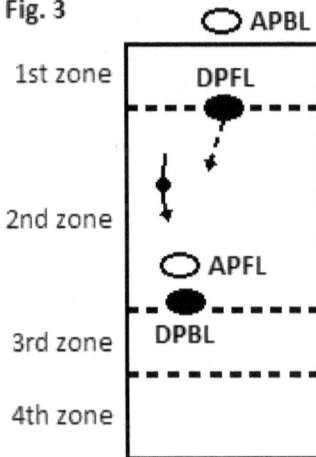

**Fig. 4**

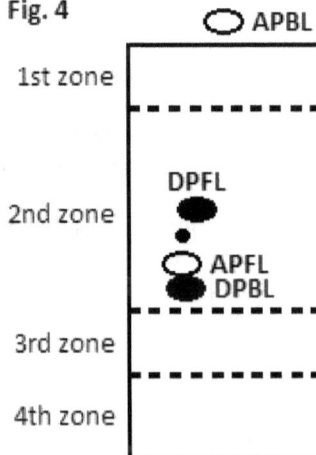

Task 1 continuation

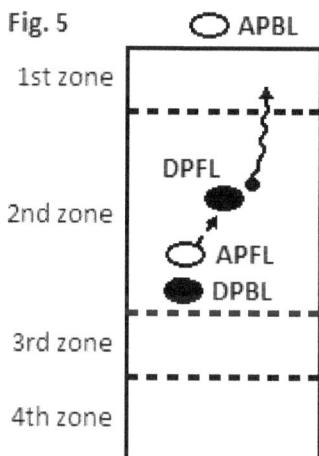

Fig. 5

1st zone

2nd zone

3rd zone

4th zone

APBL · DPFL · APFL · DPBL

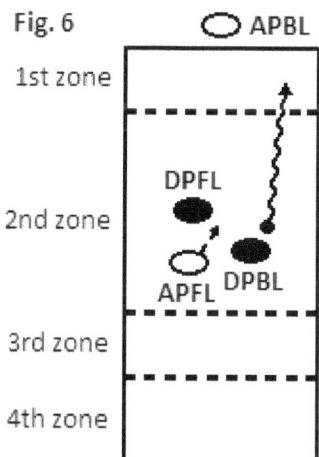

Fig. 6

1st zone

2nd zone

3rd zone

4th zone

APBL · DPFL · APFL · DPBL

**Variant:** points of initial position of the attacking player of a back line across the width of the pitch and trajectories of his passes to the partner (with a mounted trajectory, with a rebound off the pitch) are varied

**Task 2. Moving forward for tackling the ball from the attacking player, moving back after performing of a lengthwise pass by this player and squeezing in a vise the attacking player, to whom the ball was sent, with another defending player**

| Task description | Requirements for task performance quality |
|---|---|
| Playground 20 meters long and 10 meters wide is marked, divided into three zones:<br>– the first – 7 meters long;<br>– the second – 5 meters long;<br>– the third – 8 meters long;<br>The goal 6x2 meters is mounted on the short side of the playground in the third zone.<br>Two attacking and two defending players are situated:<br>– the attacking player of a front line (APFL) – in the zone 5 meters long back to the goal;<br>– the attacking player of a back line (APBL) with the ball – beyond the playground at its short side distant relative to the goal face to the goal;<br>– the defending player of a front line (DPFL) – at the line between the first and the second zones of the pitch back to the goal;<br>– the defending player of a back line (DPBL) – at the line between the second and the third zones back to the goal (fig. 1).<br>On a signal the defending player of a front line begins to go at the attacking player of a back line quickly.<br>At this moment the attacking player of a front line begins to open in the second zone of the pitch for receiving the ball, changing the direction of movement and using dummies. | – after a signal on beginning of a task performance the defending player of a back line should move towards the attacking player of a back line quickly, preventing him from passing to the attacking player of a front line;<br>– while controlling actions of the attacking player of a front line, the defending player should not enter the second zone of the pitch until the moment of performing a pass to this player and should see actions of the attacking player possessing the ball with that;<br>– the attacking players with the ball and without it should act simultaneously; |

Task 2 continuation

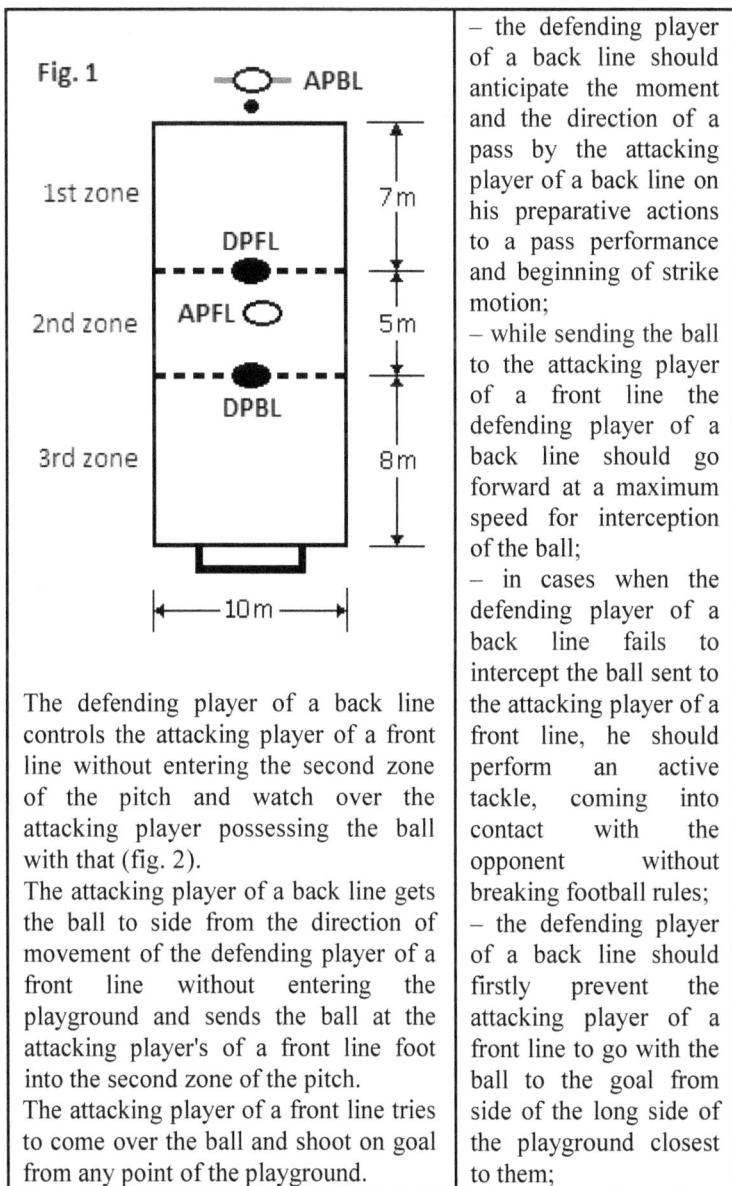

Fig. 1

○ APBL
●

1st zone — 7 m

DPFL ●

APFL ○ — 5 m

2nd zone

DPBL ●

3rd zone — 8 m

|◄— 10 m —►|

The defending player of a back line controls the attacking player of a front line without entering the second zone of the pitch and watch over the attacking player possessing the ball with that (fig. 2).

The attacking player of a back line gets the ball to side from the direction of movement of the defending player of a front line without entering the playground and sends the ball at the attacking player's of a front line foot into the second zone of the pitch.

The attacking player of a front line tries to come over the ball and shoot on goal from any point of the playground.

– the defending player of a back line should anticipate the moment and the direction of a pass by the attacking player of a back line on his preparative actions to a pass performance and beginning of strike motion;

– while sending the ball to the attacking player of a front line the defending player of a back line should go forward at a maximum speed for interception of the ball;

– in cases when the defending player of a back line fails to intercept the ball sent to the attacking player of a front line, he should perform an active tackle, coming into contact with the opponent without breaking football rules;

– the defending player of a back line should firstly prevent the attacking player of a front line to go with the ball to the goal from side of the long side of the playground closest to them;

## Task 2 continuation

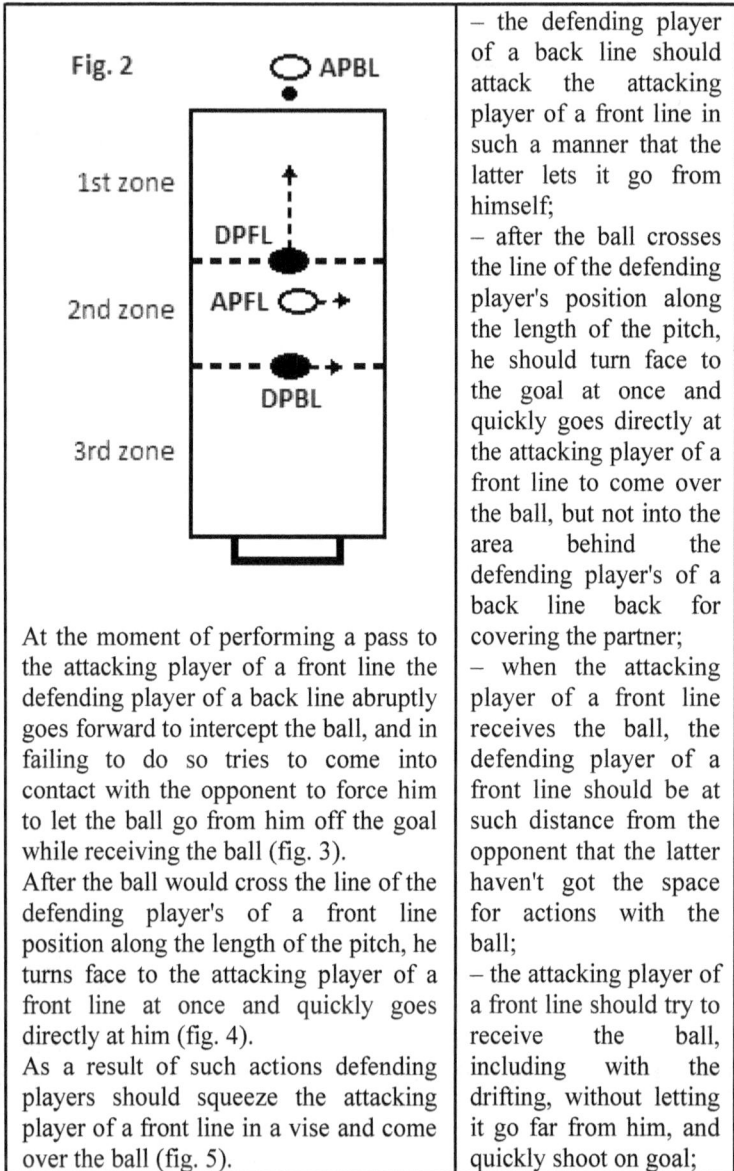

Fig. 2

APBL

1st zone

DPFL

2nd zone    APFL

DPBL

3rd zone

At the moment of performing a pass to the attacking player of a front line the defending player of a back line abruptly goes forward to intercept the ball, and in failing to do so tries to come into contact with the opponent to force him to let the ball go from him off the goal while receiving the ball (fig. 3).

After the ball would cross the line of the defending player's of a front line position along the length of the pitch, he turns face to the attacking player of a front line at once and quickly goes directly at him (fig. 4).

As a result of such actions defending players should squeeze the attacking player of a front line in a vise and come over the ball (fig. 5).

– the defending player of a back line should attack the attacking player of a front line in such a manner that the latter lets it go from himself;

– after the ball crosses the line of the defending player's position along the length of the pitch, he should turn face to the goal at once and quickly goes directly at the attacking player of a front line to come over the ball, but not into the area behind the defending player's of a back line back for covering the partner;

– when the attacking player of a front line receives the ball, the defending player of a front line should be at such distance from the opponent that the latter haven't got the space for actions with the ball;

– the attacking player of a front line should try to receive the ball, including with the drifting, without letting it go far from him, and quickly shoot on goal;

## Task 2 continuation

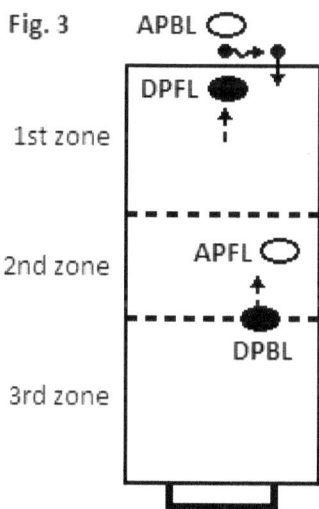

Fig. 3

1st zone

2nd zone

3rd zone

– the defending player who has come over the ball should get it through the short side of the playground distant relative to the goal beyond the playground at a maximum speed;

– the attacking player of a back line trying to prevent the defending player from getting the ball beyond the playground, should not act with a maximum activity

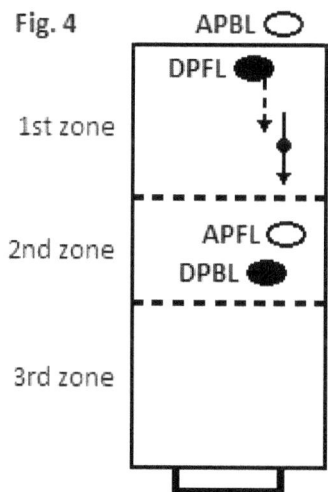

Fig. 4

1st zone

2nd zone

3rd zone

Task 2 continuation

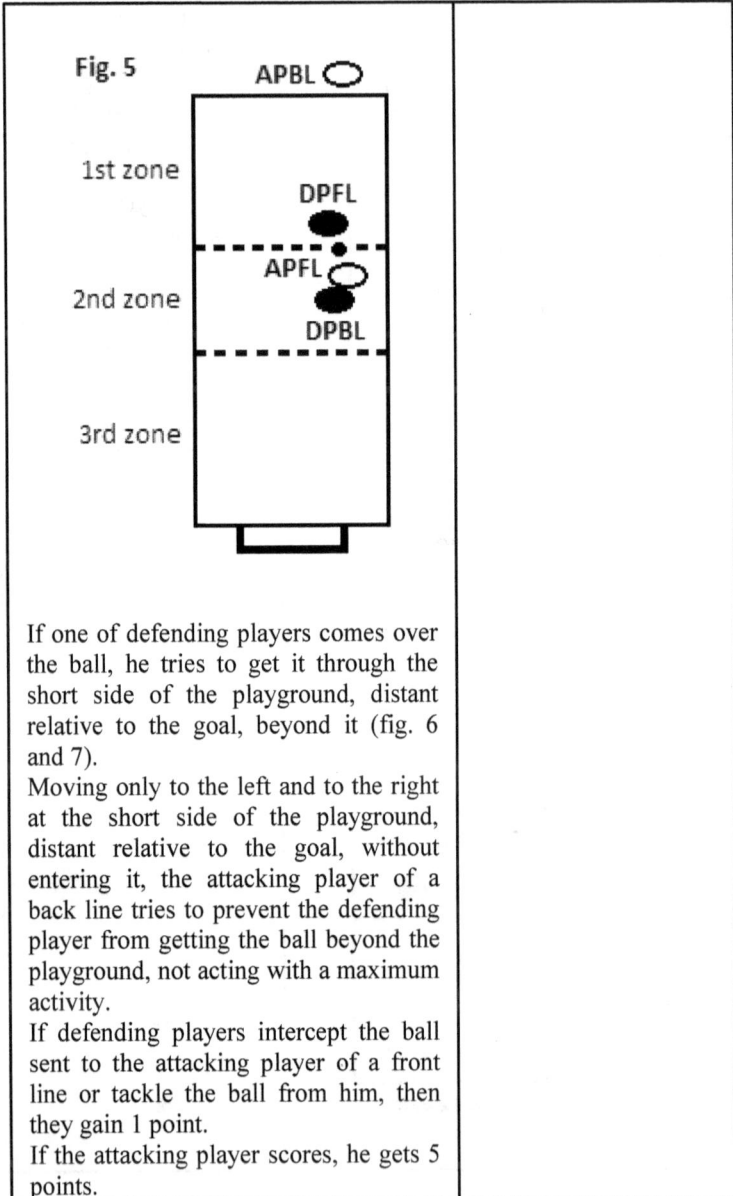

Fig. 5

APBL

1st zone

DPFL

APFL

2nd zone

DPBL

3rd zone

If one of defending players comes over the ball, he tries to get it through the short side of the playground, distant relative to the goal, beyond it (fig. 6 and 7).

Moving only to the left and to the right at the short side of the playground, distant relative to the goal, without entering it, the attacking player of a back line tries to prevent the defending player from getting the ball beyond the playground, not acting with a maximum activity.

If defending players intercept the ball sent to the attacking player of a front line or tackle the ball from him, then they gain 1 point.

If the attacking player scores, he gets 5 points.

Task 2 continuation

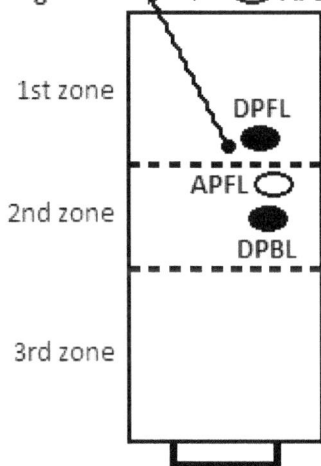

Fig. 6

1st zone

2nd zone

3rd zone

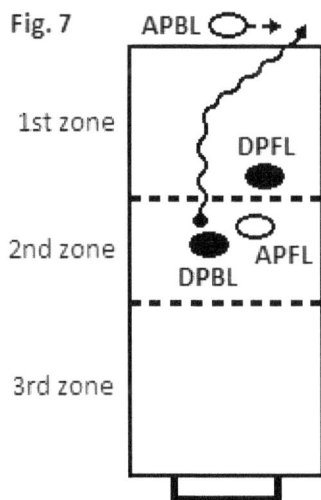

Fig. 7

1st zone

2nd zone

3rd zone

**Variant:** points of the attacking player's of a back line initial position across the width of the pitch are varied

# 7. 3. Drills for learning actions while passing the ball on the attacking player's way

**Task 1. Moving back after performing a lengthwise pass by the attacking player into the area behind another defending player's back, and coming over the ball at 7-10 meters from this defending player who has knocked the ball away from the goal**

| Task description | Requirements for task performance quality |
|---|---|
| Playground 25 meters long and 10 meters wide is marked, divided into three zones:<br>– the first – 5 meters long;<br>– the second – 10 meters long;<br>– the third – 10 meters long;<br>The goal 6x2 meters is mounted on the short side of the playground in the third zone.<br>One attacking and two defending players are situated:<br>– the attacking player with the ball – beyond the playground at its short side distant relative to the goal face to the goal;<br>– the defending player of a front line (DPFL) – at the line between the first and the second zones of the pitch back to the goal;<br>– the defending player of a back line (DPBL) – at the line between the second and the third zones back to the goal (fig. 1). | – the attacking player should send the ball into the net with a mounted trajectory with a shot of medium power and not with a powerful shot with a linear trajectory;<br>– the defending player of a back line should anticipate the moment and the direction of a pass by the attacking player on his preparative actions to a pass performance and beginning of strike motion;<br>– the defending player of a back line should quickly move back;<br>– the defending player of a front line should quickly define the trajectory of the ball sent by the attacking player; |

Task 1 continuation

**Fig. 1**

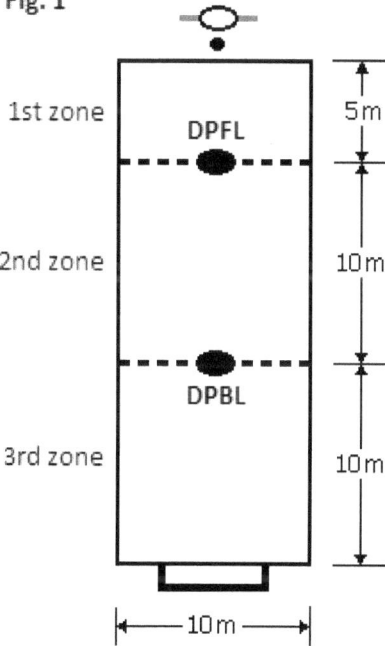

1st zone

DPFL

5 m

2nd zone

10 m

DPBL

3rd zone

10 m

|← 10 m →|

The attacking player sends the ball with a mounted trajectory into the net with a medium speed from the outside of the playground.

When the attacking player begins to perform a pass, the defending player of a back line begins to move back, moving backwards or half-sideways forward.

After the ball would cross the line of the defending player's of a front line position along the length of the pitch, he turns face to the goal at once and quickly moves towards the third zone of the pitch (fig. 2).

– after the ball would cross the line of the defending player's of a front line position along the length of the pitch, he turns face to the goal at once and quickly moves towards the third zone of the pitch to come over the ball;

– the defending player of a back line should quickly define the direction of the ball sent into the net and knock it out to the second zone of the pitch, preventing from crossing the goal-line;

– the defending player of a front line should come over the ball preventing it from crossing the line between the second and the third zones of the pitch

Task 1 continuation

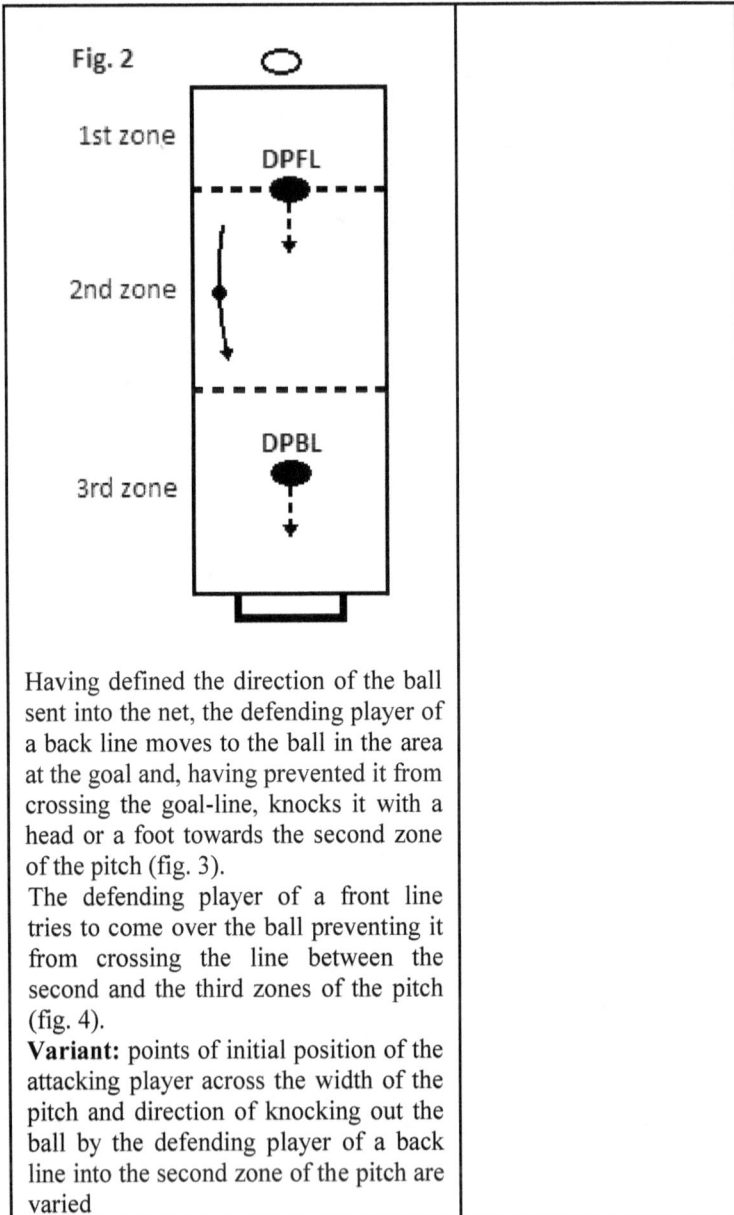

**Fig. 2**

1st zone

DPFL

2nd zone

3rd zone

DPBL

Having defined the direction of the ball sent into the net, the defending player of a back line moves to the ball in the area at the goal and, having prevented it from crossing the goal-line, knocks it with a head or a foot towards the second zone of the pitch (fig. 3).

The defending player of a front line tries to come over the ball preventing it from crossing the line between the second and the third zones of the pitch (fig. 4).

**Variant:** points of initial position of the attacking player across the width of the pitch and direction of knocking out the ball by the defending player of a back line into the second zone of the pitch are varied

Task 1 continuation

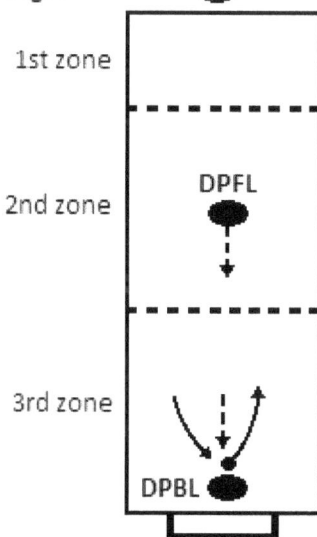

Fig. 3

1st zone

2nd zone

DPFL

3rd zone

DPBL

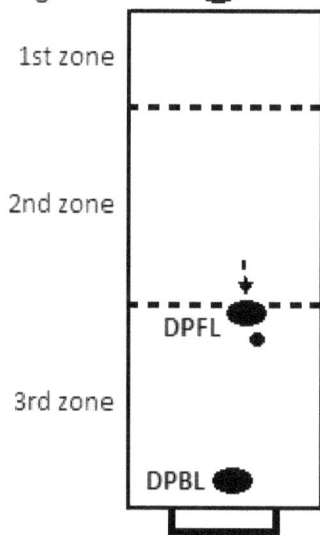

Fig. 4

1st zone

2nd zone

DPFL

3rd zone

DPBL

**Task 2. Moving back after performing a lengthwise pass by the attacking player into the area behind another defending player's back, and beating the attacking player who tries to come over the ball that was knocked out by the defending player away from the goal**

| Task description | Requirements for task performance quality |
|---|---|
| Playground 25 meters long and 10 meters wide is marked, divided into three zones:<br>– the first – 5 meters long;<br>– the second - 10 meters long;<br>– the third – 10 meters long;<br>The goal 6x2 meters is mounted on the short side of the playground in the third zone.<br>Two attacking and two defending players are situated:<br>– the attacking player of a front line (APFL) – at the point of intersection of the line between the second and the third zones of the pitch and the long side of the playground beyond it;<br>– the attacking player of a back line (APBL) with the ball – beyond the playground at its short side distant relative to the goal face to the goal;<br>– the defending player of a front line (DPFL) – at the line between the first and the second zones of the pitch back to the goal;<br>– the defending player of a back line (DPBL) – at the line between the second and the third zones back to the goal (fig. 1).<br>The attacking player sends the ball with a mounted trajectory into the net with a medium speed from the outside of the playground. | – the attacking player of a back line should send the ball into the net with a mounted trajectory with a shot of medium power and not with a powerful shot with a linear trajectory;<br>– the defending player of a back line should anticipate the moment and the direction of a pass by the attacking player of a back line on his preparative actions to a pass performance and beginning of strike motion;<br>– the defending player of a front line should quickly define the trajectory of the ball sent by the attacking player of a back line;<br>– the defending player of a back line should quickly move back; |

Task 2 continuation

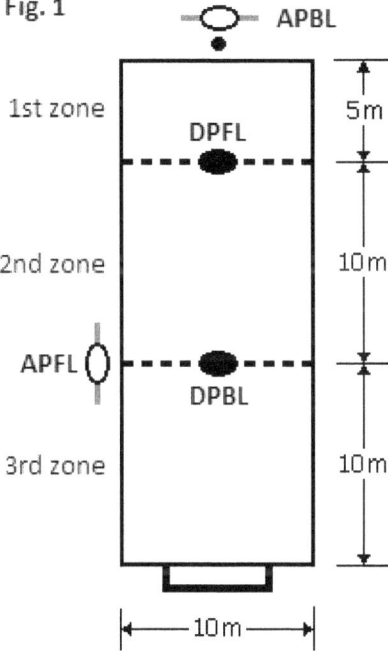

**Fig. 1**

APBL

1st zone       5m

DPFL

2nd zone       10m

APFL

DPBL

3rd zone       10m

|←——10m——→|

When the attacking player begins to perform a pass, the defending player of a back line begins to move back, moving backwards or half-sideways forward.

After the ball would cross the line of the defending player's of a front line position along the length of the pitch, he turns face to the goal at once and quickly moves towards the third zone of the pitch (fig. 2).

– after the ball would cross the line of the defending player's of a front line position along the length of the pitch, he turns face to the goal at once and quickly moves towards the partner to come over the ball;

– the defending player of a back line should quickly define the direction of the ball sent into the net and knock it out to the defending player of a front line, preventing the ball from crossing the goal-line;

– the attacking player of a front line should begin to move into the playground only at the moment of knocking the ball out by the defending player of a back line;

– trying to come over the ball, the attacking player of a front line should not to act with a maximum activity;

– the defending player of a front line should come over the ball regardless of direction and trajectory of the ball sent by partner

Task 2 continuation

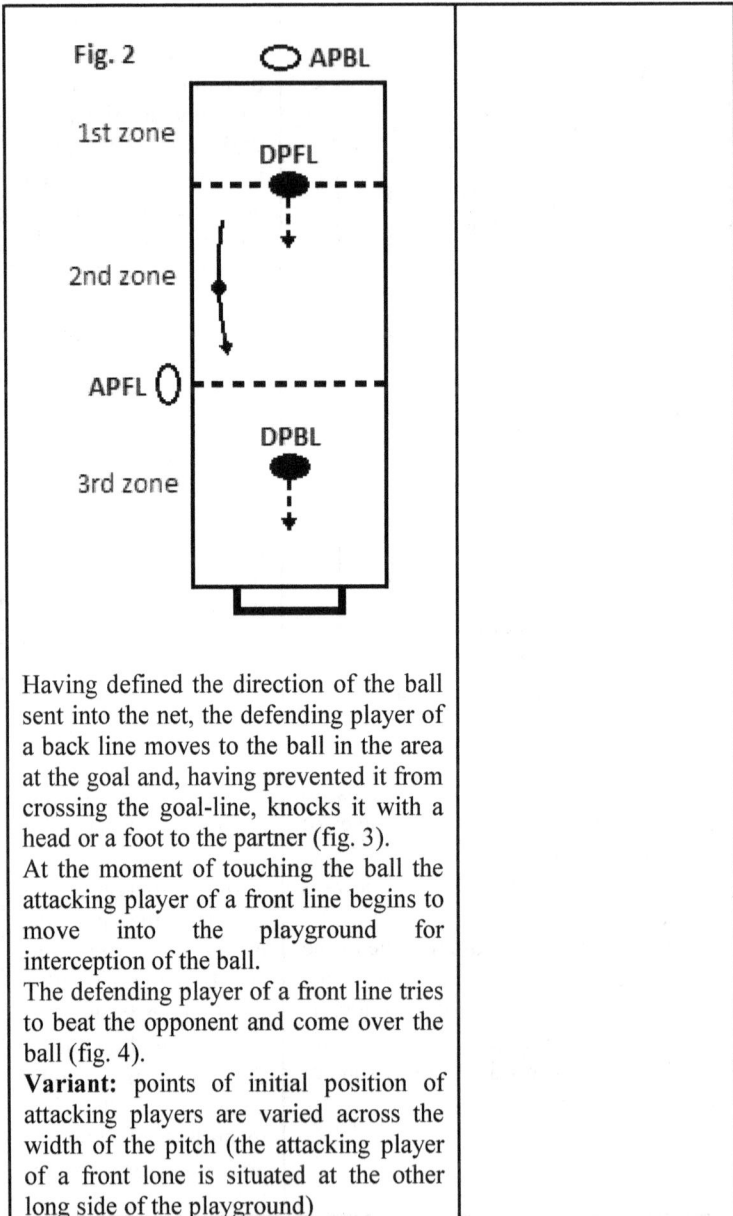

Fig. 2

APBL

1st zone

DPFL

2nd zone

APFL

DPBL

3rd zone

Having defined the direction of the ball sent into the net, the defending player of a back line moves to the ball in the area at the goal and, having prevented it from crossing the goal-line, knocks it with a head or a foot to the partner (fig. 3).

At the moment of touching the ball the attacking player of a front line begins to move into the playground for interception of the ball.

The defending player of a front line tries to beat the opponent and come over the ball (fig. 4).

**Variant:** points of initial position of attacking players are varied across the width of the pitch (the attacking player of a front lone is situated at the other long side of the playground)

Task 2 continuation

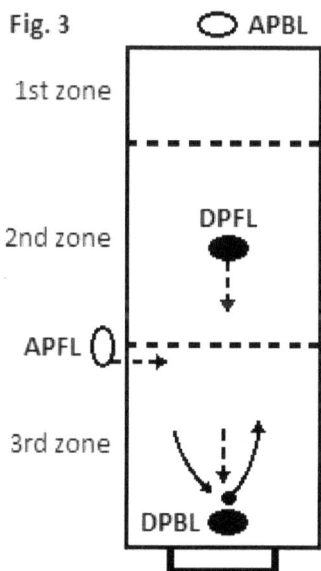

**Fig. 3**

APBL

1st zone

2nd zone

DPFL

APFL

3rd zone

DPBL

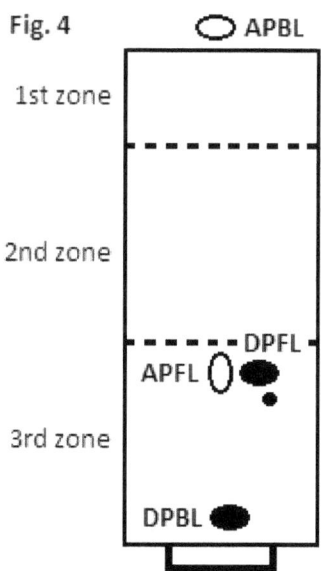

**Fig. 4**

APBL

1st zone

2nd zone

DPFL

APFL

3rd zone

DPBL

# CHAPTER 8.
# GAMING DRILL FOR LEARNING
# THE BASIC ELEMENTS
# OF ZONAL PRESSING TACTICS

## 8. 1. Characteristics of construction of gaming drills with the contiguous goals

Learning different tactical skills of football may be considered successful, if players begin to apply these skills in games fairly effective. It is completely subject to learning basic elements of zonal pressing tactics by players.

The number of cases and quality of performance of one or other tactical techniques are largely due to the fact if gaming drills were used while learning. This is due to that these drills are specific bridge while transition from conditions of drills in which footballers' actions are strictly defined in advance to conditions of real situations occurring in competitive games.

Basic elements of zonal pressing tactics are individual actions and interactions of two defending players.

In this regard gaming drills performed with a little number of players in teams on the pitches of reduced size with the contiguous goals of standard size are effective for learning these actions. This is due to the fact that on course of such drills certain play situations are set up frequently, and players may perform one or another tactical actions specific for zonal pressing.

There may be marked several characteristics in constructing of gaming drills with the contiguous goals in cases of using it for learning basic elements of zonal pressing tactics.

**First.** Optimum number of in-field players in teams-from one to seven.

**Second.** Some drills may be used while learning certain basic elements of zonal pressing tactics and performed with the participation of one to three players in each team.

In other drills there may be four to seven players in teams and may be visible main play lines (defense, midfield and attack) peculiar to football that allows training all basic elements of zonal pressing tactics as a whole.

**Third.** Using certain organization of gaming drills with the contiguous goals there may be created conditions for consolidation of those tactical skills peculiar to zonal pressing, learning of which is the main task at the moment.

For example, putting into drill the «neutral» player acting for whose possessing the ball all the time would allow footballers to learn skills of controlling attacking players not possessing the ball faster. Refusal to abide the offside rule at first time would force defending players to position themselves properly relative to the opponent not possessing the ball.

**Fourth.** Number of cases when certain tactical skills are performed might be increased by means of certain objectives to players how to act in one or another situations.

**Fifth.** While using gaming drills with the contiguous goals for learning basic elements of zonal pressing tactics by young footballers the goal should be compatible with players' capabilities. Particularly the goal 6x2 meters is optimal for kids 10-12 y.o., whereas at 13 and older – the goal of standard size.

# 8. 2. Gaming drills with the contiguous goals for learning certain basic elements of zonal pressing tactics

**Task 1. One on one play into two goals protected by goalkeepers for defending players' learning actions in «one on the attacking player without the ball, situated in front of him along the length of the pitch» situations**

| Task description | Requirements for task performance quality |
|---|---|
| Pitch size: 10 meters wide, 25 meters long. Middle zone 15 meters long and the goal area not far than 5 meters from the goal-line are marked on the pitch.<br>In initial position players are situated in the middle zone of the pitch.<br><br> | – the attacking player should move for receiving the ball with an ultimate output, changing the direction of movement and using dummies;<br>– up to the moment of sending the ball to the attacking player the defending player should be 2-3 meters from him and see goalkeepers' actions with the ball with that;<br>– goalkeepers should timely sent it to a partner at foot or on a way depending on situation; |

Task 1 continuation

| | |
|---|---|
| On signal goalkeepers put the ball into play to the middle zone of the pitch after catching it or when it has left the field through the goal-line or sidelines. Moving along the length and across the width of the pitch, the attacking player tries to receive the ball in the middle zone and shoot on goal.<br><br>The defending player tries to intercept the ball or tackle it from the attacking player and shoot on goal.<br><br>The attacking player gets 1 extra point if comes over the ball sent at his foot, and 3 points if receives the ball in space behind the defending player's back.<br><br>While playing in defense players get keynote to act in following manner:<br>– to control the attacking player without the ball being 2-3 meters from him before the moment of sending the ball to him;<br>– to prevent the attacking player's attempts to come over the ball firstly in space behind the defending player's back;<br>– to go into active tackle if the attacking player is successful in coming over the ball.<br><br>Goalkeepers are prohibited to play outside the goal area.<br><br>Corners are not awarded.<br><br>**Offsides are not given.**<br><br>Players are permitted to pass the ball to goalkeepers only when putting it into play after fouls.<br><br>Play time in one repeat – 1-1,5 minutes | – the defending player should anticipate the moment and the direction of a pass by the goalkeeper on his preparative actions to a pass performance and beginning of strike motion;<br>– during sending the ball on the attacking player's way the defending player should always be first on the ball;<br>– while sending the ball at the attacking player's foot the defending player should go forward at a maximum speed for interception of the ball;<br>– in case the attacking player comes over the ball the defending player should begin active tackling along the playground, entering into physical contact with the opponent |

**Task 2. Two on two play into two goals protected by goalkeepers for defending players' learning actions in «one on the attacking player without the ball, situated in front of him along the length of the pitch» situations, and two on the attacking player moving with the ball towards them along the length of the pitch**

| Task description | Requirements for task performance quality |
|---|---|
| Pitch size: 18 meters wide, 20 meters long. Middle zone 10 meters long and the goal area not far than 5 meters from the goal-line are marked on the pitch. In initial position players are situated in the middle zone of the pitch.<br><br><br><br>On signal goalkeepers put the ball into play to the middle zone of the pitch after catching it or when it has left the field through the goal-line or sidelines. Moving along the length and across the width of the pitch, attacking players try to receive the ball in the middle zone and shoot on goal. | – attacking players should move for receiving the ball with an ultimate output, changing the direction of movement and using dummies; <br>– until the moment when the ball is sent to attacking players defending players should be situated each subsequently 2-3 meters from the attacking player situated in their zone if responsibility and see the goalkeeper's actions with the ball with that; <br>– goalkeepers should timely sent it to partners at foot or on a way depending on situation; <br>– defending players should anticipate the moment and the direction of a pass by the goalkeeper on his preparative actions to a pass performance and beginning of strike motion; |

## Task 2 continuation

| | |
|---|---|
| Defending players try to intercept the ball or tackle it from attacking players and shoot on goal.<br><br>Attacking players get 1 extra point if come over the ball sent at their foot by the goalkeeper, and 3 points if receive the ball from the goalkeeper in space behind defending players' back.<br><br>While playing in defense players get keynote to act in following manner:<br><br>– to control the attacking player without the ball in their zone of responsibility being 2-3 meters from him before the moment of sending the ball to him;<br><br>– to prevent attacking players' attempts to come over the ball firstly in space behind defending players' back;<br><br>– to go into active tackle if the attacking player is successful in coming over the ball and to eliminate a possibility of the opponent coming forward with the ball from the side distant relative to the second defending player;<br><br>– to cover each other in attempts to intercept and tackle the ball by one of defending players.<br><br>Goalkeepers are prohibited to play outside the goal area.<br><br>Corners are not awarded.<br><br>**Offsides are not given.**<br><br>Players are permitted to pass the ball to goalkeepers only when putting it into play after fouls.<br><br>Play time in one repeat – 2,5-3 minutes | – defending players should go forward at a maximum speed to intercept the ball sent at the attacking player's foot and always be first at the ball sent on the attacking player's way;<br><br>– in case the attacking player comes over the ball one defending player should begin active tackling along the playground, entering into physical contact with the opponent, and another should cover the partner |

**Task 3. Two on two play into two goals protected by goalkeepers, with the neutral player acting for those possessing the ball, for defending player's learning actions in situations «two on the attacking player without the ball, situated in front of them along the length of the pitch», and «two on the attacking player moving with the ball towards them along the length of the pitch»**

| Task description | Requirements for task performance quality |
|---|---|
| Pitch size: 20 meters wide, 20 meters long. Middle zone 10 meters long and the goal area not far than 5 meters from the goal-line are marked on the pitch. In initial position players are situated in the middle zone of the pitch. On signal goalkeepers put the ball into play to the middle zone of the pitch after catching it or when it has left the field through the goal-line or sidelines. | – attacking players should move for receiving the ball with an ultimate output, changing the direction of movement and using dummies; – until the moment when the ball is sent to attacking players defending players should be situated each subsequently 2-3 meters from the attacking player situated in their zone if responsibility and see the goalkeeper's actions with the ball with that; – goalkeepers should timely sent it to partners at foot or on a way depending on situation; |

Task 3 continuation

| | |
|---|---|
| Moving along the length and across the width of the pitch, attacking players try to receive the ball in the middle zone and shoot on goal. Defending players try to intercept the ball or tackle it from attacking players and shoot on goal. Attacking players get 1 extra point if come over the ball sent at their foot by the goalkeeper, and 3 points if receive the ball from the goalkeeper in space behind defending players' back. While playing in defense players get keynote to act in following manner: – to control the attacking player without the ball in their zone of responsibility being 2-3 meters from him before the moment of sending the ball to him; – to prevent attacking players' attempts to come over the ball firstly in space behind defending players' back; – to go into active tackle if the attacking player is successful in coming over the ball and to eliminate a possibility of the opponent coming forward with the ball from the side distant relative to the second defending player; – to cover each other in attempts to intercept and tackle the ball by one of defending players. Goalkeepers are prohibited to play outside the goal area. Corners are not awarded. **Offsides are not given.** Players are permitted to pass the ball to goalkeepers only when putting it into play after fouls. Play time in one repeat – 2,5-3 minutes | – defending players should anticipate the moment and the direction of a pass by the goalkeeper on his preparative actions to a pass performance and beginning of strike motion; – defending players should go forward at a maximum speed to intercept the ball sent at the attacking player's foot and always be first at the ball sent on the attacking player's way; – in case the attacking player comes over the ball one defending player should begin active tackling along the playground, entering into physical contact with the opponent, and another should cover the partner |

**Task 4. Three on three play into two goals protected by goalkeepers, for defending players' learning actions in situations «two on the attacking player without the ball situated in front of them along the length of the pitch», and «two on the attacking player moving with the ball towards them along the length of the pitch»**

| Task description | Requirements for task performance quality |
|---|---|
| Pitch size: 20 meters wide, 25 meters long. Half-way line dividing the pitch into attacking and defensive zones is marked. In initial position players are situated in the defensive zone of the team which goalkeepers puts the ball into play. On signal goalkeepers put the ball into play after catching it or when it has left the field through the goal-line or sidelines, or to their defensive zone (at the partner's foot) or attacking zone (on the partner's way). | – attacking players should move for receiving the ball with an ultimate output, changing the direction of movement and using dummies; – until the moment when the ball is sent to attacking players defending players should be situated each subsequently 2-3 meters from the attacking player situated in their zone if responsibility and see the goalkeeper's actions with the ball with that; – defending players should anticipate the moment of performance and directions of opponents' passes; |

Task 4 continuation

| | |
|---|---|
| Moving along the length and across the width of the pitch, attacking players try to receive the ball in their defensive or attacking zone and shoot on goal. | – defending players should go forward at a maximum speed to intercept the ball sent at the attacking player's foot and always be first at the ball sent on the attacking player's way; |
| Defending players try to intercept the ball or tackle it from attacking players and shoot on goal. | |
| Attacking players get 1 extra point if come over the ball sent at their foot by the goalkeeper, and 3 points if receive the ball from the goalkeeper in the attacking zone or from the partner from defensive zone. | – in case the attacking player comes over the ball one defending player should begin active tackling along the playground, entering into physical contact with the opponent, and partners should cover him; |
| While playing in defense players get keynote to act in following manner: | |
| – to control the attacking player without the ball in their zone of responsibility being 2-3 meters from him before the moment of sending the ball to him; | |
| – to prevent attacking players' attempts to come over the ball firstly in space behind defending players' back; | – defending players should not try to create an offside while attacking players' attempts to receive the ball in the attacking zone; |
| – to go into active tackle if the attacking player is successful in coming over the ball and to eliminate a possibility of the opponent coming with the ball into the attacking zone from the side of sideline closest to the ball; | – defending players should timely press attacking players out from their half of the pitch |
| – to cover each other in attempts to intercept and tackle the ball by one of defending players. | |
| Corners are not awarded. | |
| **Offsides are not given.** | |
| Play time in one repeat – 4-5 minutes | |

**Task 5. Three on three play into two goals protected by goalkeepers, with the neutral player acting for those possessing the ball, for defending player's learning actions in situations «two on the attacking player without the ball, situated in front of them along the length of the pitch», and «two on the attacking player moving with the ball towards them along the length of the pitch»**

| Task description | Requirements for task performance quality |
|---|---|
| Pitch size: 20 meters wide, 25 meters long. Half-way line dividing the pitch into attacking and defensive zones is marked. In initial position players are situated in the defensive zone of the team which goalkeepers puts the ball into play. On signal goalkeepers put the ball into play after catching it or when it has left the field through the goal-line or sidelines, or to their defensive zone or attacking zone (on the partner's way). | – attacking players should move for receiving the ball with an ultimate output, changing the direction of movement and using dummies; – until the moment when the ball is sent to attacking players defending players should be situated each subsequently 2-3 meters from the attacking player situated in their zone if responsibility and see the goalkeeper's actions with the ball with that; – defending players should anticipate the moment of performance and directions of opponents' passes; |

Task 5 continuation

| | |
|---|---|
| Moving along the length and across the width of the pitch, attacking players try to receive the ball in their defensive or attacking zone and shoot on goal. Defending players try to intercept the ball or tackle it from attacking players and shoot on goal. Attacking players get 1 extra point if come over the ball sent at their foot by the goalkeeper, and 3 points if receive the ball from the goalkeeper in the attacking zone or from the partner from defensive zone. While playing in defense players get keynote to act in following manner: – to control the attacking player without the ball in their zone of responsibility being 2-3 meters from him before the moment of sending the ball to him; – to prevent attacking players' attempts to come over the ball firstly in space behind defending players' back; – to go into active tackle if the attacking player is successful in coming over the ball and to eliminate a possibility of the opponent coming with the ball into the attacking zone from the side of sideline closest to the ball; – to cover each other in attempts to intercept and tackle the ball by one of defending players. Corners are not awarded. **Offsides are not given.** Play time in one repeat – 4-5 minutes | – defending players should go forward at a maximum speed to intercept the ball sent at the attacking player's foot and always be first at the ball sent on the attacking player's way; – in case the attacking player comes over the ball one defending player should begin active tackling along the playground, entering into physical contact with the opponent, and partners should cover him; – defending players should not try to create an offside while attacking players' attempts to receive the ball in the attacking zone; – defending players should timely press attacking players out from their half of the pitch |

## 8. 3. Gaming drills with the contiguous goals for learning all basic elements of zonal pressing tactics as a whole

**Task 1. Four on four play into two goals protected by goalkeepers, with two defenders in scheme 2- 1- 1 (two defenders – one midfielder – one striker)**

| Task description | Requirements for task performance quality |
|---|---|
| Pitch size: 20 meters wide, 35 meters long.<br><br><br><br>Goalkeepers put the ball into play after catching it or when it crosses the goal-line from players of the attacking team. | – while switching of one of defenders into the attack the second one should necessarily cover the partner;<br>– until the moment when the ball is sent to attacking players defending players should be situated each subsequently 2-3 meters from the attacking player situated in their zone if responsibility and see the actions of opponent with the ball with that;<br>– defending players should anticipate the moment of performance and directions of opponents' passes; |

Task 1 continuation

Corners are awarded.
While playing in attack defenders get keynote to act in following manner:
– one of defenders should participate in each attack alternately, moving forward with the ball or without it;
– while switching of one of defenders into attack the second one should move to the central lengthwise axis of the pitch for covering him.
While playing in defense players get keynote to act in following manner:
– to control the attacking player without the ball in their zone of responsibility being 2-3 meters from him before the moment of sending the ball to him;
– to prevent attacking players' attempts to come over the ball firstly in space behind defending players' back;
– to go into active tackle if the attacking player is successful in coming over the ball and to eliminate a possibility of the opponent coming with the ball forward from the side of sideline closest to the ball;
– to squeeze the opponent in a vise if the ball is sent to the attacking player situated between defending players of different play lines;
– to cover each other in attempts to intercept and tackle the ball by one of defending players.
**Offsides are not given.**
Play time in one repeat – 5 minutes

– defending players should go forward at a maximum speed to intercept the ball sent at the attacking player's foot and always be first at the ball sent on the attacking player's way;
– in case the attacking player comes over the ball one defending player should begin active tackling along the playground, entering into physical contact with the opponent, and partners should cover him;
– defending players of different play lines should squeeze in a vise the attacking player situated in front of them along the length of the pitch while the ball is sent to him;
– defending players should observe necessary compact arrangement

**Task 2. Five on five play into two goals protected by goalkeepers, two defenders in scheme 2- 2- 1 (two defenders – two midfielders – one striker) or 2 - 1- 2 (two defenders – one midfielder – two strikers)**

| Task description | Requirements for task performance quality |
|---|---|
| Pitch size: 25 meters wide, 40 meters long. Half-way line dividing the pitch in two is marked.<br><br><br><br>Goalkeepers put the ball into play after catching it or when it crosses the goal-line from players of the attacking team.<br>If the ball leaves the pitch through the touchlines, it is put into play by players. | – while switching of one of defenders into the attack the second one should necessarily cover the partner;<br>– until the moment when the ball is sent to attacking players defending players should be situated each subsequently 2-3 meters from the attacking player situated in their zone if responsibility and see the actions of opponent with the ball with that;<br>– defending players should anticipate the moment of performance and directions of opponents' passes;<br>– defending players should observe necessary compact arrangement; |

Task 2 continuation

Corners are awarded.

While playing in attack defenders get keynote to act in following manner:

– one of defenders should participate in attacks alternately, moving forward with the ball or without it;

– while switching of one of defenders into attack the second one should move to the central lengthwise axis of the pitch for covering him.

While playing in defense players get keynote to act in following manner:

– to control the attacking player without the ball in their zone of responsibility being 2-3 meters from him before the moment of sending the ball to him;

– to prevent attacking players' attempts to come over the ball firstly in space behind defending players' back;

– to go into active tackle if the attacking player is successful in coming over the ball and to eliminate a possibility of the opponent coming with the ball forward from the side of sideline closest to the ball;

– to squeeze the opponent in a vise if the ball is sent to the attacking player situated between defending players of different play lines;

– to cover each other in attempts to intercept and tackle the ball by one of defending players.

**Offsides are given.**

Play time in one repeat – 5-7 minutes

– defending players should go forward at a maximum speed to intercept the ball sent at the attacking player's foot and always be first at the ball sent on the attacking player's way;

– in case the attacking player comes over the ball one defending player should begin active tackling along the playground, entering into physical contact with the opponent, and partners should cover him;

– defending players of different play lines should squeeze in a vise the attacking player situated in front of them along the length of the pitch while the ball is sent to him;

– defending players should timely press attacking players out from their half of the pitch

**Task 3. Six on six play into two goals protected by goalkeepers, with two defenders in scheme 2- 3- 1 (two defenders – three midfielders – one striker) or 2 - 2 - 1 - 1 (two defenders – two midfielders – one inside – one striker)**

| Task description | Requirements for task performance quality |
|---|---|
| Pitch size: 30 meters wide, 50 meters long. Half-way line dividing the pitch in two is marked. | – while switching of one of defenders into the attack the second one should necessarily cover the partner;<br>– until the moment when the ball is sent to attacking players defending players should be situated each subsequently 2-3 meters from the attacking player situated in their zone if responsibility and see the actions of opponent with the ball with that;<br>– defending players should anticipate the moment of performance and directions of opponents' passes;<br>– defending players should observe necessary compact arrangement; |
| Goalkeepers put the ball into play after catching it or when it crosses the goal-line from players of the attacking team. If the ball leaves the pitch through the touchlines, it is put into play by players. | |

Task 3 continuation

| | |
|---|---|
| Corners are awarded.<br>While playing in attack defenders get keynote to act in following manner:<br>– one of defenders should participate in attacks alternately, moving forward with the ball or without it;<br>– while switching of one of defenders into attack the second one should move to the central lengthwise axis of the pitch for covering him.<br>While playing in defense players get keynote to act in following manner:<br>– to control the attacking player without the ball in their zone of responsibility being 2-3 meters from him before the moment of sending the ball to him;<br>– to prevent attacking players' attempts to come over the ball firstly in space behind defending players' back;<br>– to go into active tackle if the attacking player is successful in coming over the ball and to eliminate a possibility of the opponent coming with the ball forward from the side of sideline closest to the ball;<br>– to squeeze the opponent in a vise if the ball is sent to the attacking player situated between defending players of different play lines;<br>– to cover each other in attempts to intercept and tackle the ball by one of defending players.<br>**Offsides are given.**<br>Play time in one repeat – 8-10 minutes | – defending players should go forward at a maximum speed to intercept the ball sent at the attacking player's foot and always be first at the ball sent on the attacking player's way;<br>– in case the attacking player comes over the ball one defending player should begin active tackling along the playground, entering into physical contact with the opponent, and partners should cover him;<br>– defending players of different play lines should squeeze in a vise the attacking player situated in front of them along the length of the pitch while the ball is sent to him;<br>– defending players should timely press attacking players out from their half of the pitch |

**Task 4. Six on six play into two goals protected by goalkeepers, with two defenders in scheme 3 - 2 - 1 (three defenders – two midfielders – one striker) or 3 - 1 - 2 (three defenders – one midfielder – two strikers)**

| Task description | Requirements for task performance quality |
|---|---|
| Pitch size: 30 meters wide, 50 meters long. Half-way line dividing the pitch in two is marked.<br><br> | – while switching of one of defenders into the attack two another should necessarily cover the partner;<br>– until the moment when the ball is sent to attacking players defending players should be situated each subsequently 2-3 meters from the attacking player situated in their zone if responsibility and see the actions of opponent with the ball with that;<br>– defending players should anticipate the moment of performance and directions of opponents' passes;<br>– defending players should observe necessary compact arrangement; |
| Goalkeepers put the ball into play after catching it or when it crosses the goal-line from players of the attacking team. If the ball leaves the pitch through the touchlines, it is put into play by players. | |

Task 4 continuation

| | |
|---|---|
| Corners are awarded.<br>While playing in attack defenders get keynote to act in following manner:<br>– one of defenders should participate in attacks alternately, moving forward with the ball or without it;<br>– while full-back switches into attack two another should move to the left and to the right to cover him, and if center-half does so, two another should close with each other.<br>While playing in defense players get keynote to act in following manner:<br>– to control the attacking player without the ball in their zone of responsibility being 2-3 meters from him before the moment of sending the ball to him;<br>– to prevent attacking players' attempts to come over the ball firstly in space behind defending players' back;<br>– to go into active tackle if the attacking player is successful in coming over the ball and to eliminate a possibility of the opponent coming with the ball forward from the side of sideline closest to the ball;<br>– to squeeze the opponent in a vise if the ball is sent to the attacking player situated between defending players of different play lines;<br>– to cover each other in attempts to intercept and tackle the ball by one of defending players.<br>**Offsides are given.**<br>Play time in one repeat – 10 minutes | – defending players should go forward at a maximum speed to intercept the ball sent at the attacking player's foot and always be first at the ball sent on the attacking player's way;<br>– in case the attacking player comes over the ball one defending player should begin active tackling along the playground, entering into physical contact with the opponent, and partners should cover him;<br>– defending players of different play lines should squeeze in a vise the attacking player situated in front of them along the length of the pitch while the ball is sent to him;<br>– defending players should timely press attacking players out from their half of the pitch |

**Task 5. Seven on seven play into two goals protected by goalkeepers, with three defenders in scheme 3 - 1 - 2 - 1 (three defenders – one midfielder – two insides – one striker) or 3 - 2 - 2 (three defenders – two midfielders – two strikers)**

| Task description | Requirements for task performance quality |
|---|---|
| Pitch size: 35 meters wide, 60 meters long. Half-way line dividing the pitch in two is marked.<br><br><br><br>Goalkeepers put the ball into play after catching it or when it crosses the goal-line from players of the attacking team.<br>If the ball leaves the pitch through the touchlines, it is put into play by players. | – while switching of one of defenders into the attack two another should necessarily cover the partner;<br>– until the moment when the ball is sent to attacking players defending players should be situated each subsequently 2-3 meters from the attacking player situated in their zone if responsibility and see the actions of opponent with the ball with that;<br>– defending players should anticipate the moment of performance and directions of opponents' passes;<br>– defending players should observe necessary compact arrangement; |

208

Task 5 continuation

| | |
|---|---|
| Corners are awarded.<br>While playing in attack defenders get keynote to act in following manner:<br>– one of defenders should participate in attacks alternately, moving forward with the ball or without it;<br>– while full-back switches into attack two another should move to the left and to the right to cover him, and if center-half does so, two another should close with each other.<br>While playing in defense players get keynote to act in following manner:<br>– to control the attacking player without the ball in their zone of responsibility being 2-3 meters from him before the moment of sending the ball to him;<br>– to prevent attacking players' attempts to come over the ball firstly in space behind defending players' back;<br>– to go into active tackle if the attacking player is successful in coming over the ball and to eliminate a possibility of the opponent coming with the ball forward from the side of sideline closest to the ball;<br>– to squeeze the opponent in a vise if the ball is sent to the attacking player situated between defending players of different play lines;<br>– to cover each other in attempts to intercept and tackle the ball by one of defending players.<br>**Offsides are given.**<br>Play time in one repeat – 15 minutes | – defending players should go forward at a maximum speed to intercept the ball sent at the attacking player's foot and always be first at the ball sent on the attacking player's way;<br>– in case the attacking player comes over the ball one defending player should begin active tackling along the playground, entering into physical contact with the opponent, and partners should cover him;<br>– defending players of different play lines should squeeze in a vise the attacking player situated in front of them along the length of the pitch while the ball is sent to him;<br>– defending players should timely press attacking players out from their half of the pitch |

# AFTERWORD

**First.** Drills for learning basic elements of zonal pressing tactics may be used during the work either with young players and players of professional teams. This is due to the following.

These drills were field tested in children and youth football, and, as shown by experience, it allows young footballers to move to implementation of zonal pressing tactics in 11x11 play faster and easier. Most of these exercises are quite accessible for young footballers from 11 y. o. at least.

Certain exercises for learning basic elements of zonal pressing tactics were employed also in professional teams, including in Russian Premier League teams. Experience has shown that vulnerabilities of tactical qualification of certain players may be eliminated and playing problems of team while defending actions organization may be resolved using these drills.

**Second.** While describing drills for learning basic elements of zonal pressing tactics parameters of tasks construction and requirements for players' actions relating footballers 11-13 y.o. are provided.

It is necessary to adjust organization of supposed tactical drills in each specific case depending on age and level of training of young footballers to ensure quality of task performance by players and achieving the goal of drill consequently.

Firstly the conditions of drills may vary from the point of distance and way of passes by players (with hand rather than foot), speed of footballers' movement, the value of space in which the task is performed.

**Third.** Drills suggested for learning basic elements of zonal pressing tactics differ in difficulty of performed actions and quickness of its learning by footballers.

For example, the goal of certain drills is only to familiarize players with elemental tactical actions. Anyhow these actions occur on course of drills aimed at learning more complicated (complex) individual actions and interactions as a couple.

Therefore the working time for drills the purpose of which is to familiarize players with elemental tactical actions, may be ultimately reduced.

**Fourth.** In modern football all the footballers should have defensive skills while using zonal pressing in a varying degree without reference to their play position.

Taking into account this and that changing of play position is possible at senior adolescence and even in professional team it is important that all the young footballers are schooled of zonal pressing tactics, i.e. learn its basic elements, at proper time.

**Fifth.** If players of professional team have skills of defensive play with the use of zonal pressing, then some of suggested in this book drills may be applied for correction of typical tactical mistakes in defensive individual actions and interactions of players and during the preparation of team for oncoming match.

In these cases it is necessary to define the tactical problem precisely and select those drills allowing to resolve it in a minimum of time, considering that footballers' training time is limited by the necessity of different problems solution.

# BIBLIOGRAPHY

Аверьянов А. Характеристика варианта зонного метода обороны с четырьмя защитниками / А. Аверьянов // Теория и практика футбола. – 2003. – № 2. – С. 2-6.

Аркадьев Б.А. Тактика «подвижной обороны» / Б.А. Аркадьев // В книге: Тактика футбольной игры. – М.: Физкультура и спорт, 1962. – С. 68-75.

Голомазов С.В., Чирва Б.Г. Овладение мячом при перехвате передач и отборе у соперника / С.В. Голомазов, Б.Г. Чирва // В книге: Теория и методика футбола. Том 1. Техника игры. – М.: ТВТ Дивизион, 2008. – С. 59-60.

Джоунз Р., Трэнтер Т. Футбол. Тактика защиты и нападения (пер. с англ.) / Р. Джоунз, Т. Трэнтер. – М.: ТВТ Дивизион, 2008. – 132 с.

Игнатьева В.Я. Тактика защиты / В.Я. Игнатьева // В книге: Гандбол: пособие для ин-тов физической культуры. – М.: Физкультура и спорт, 1983. – С. 57-67.

Калинин А. Игра защитников / А. Калинин. – М.: Физкультура и спорт, 1967. – 78 с.

Качалин Г.Д. Игра защитников / Г.Д. Качалин // В книге: Тактика футбола. – М.: Физкультура и спорт, 1986. – С. 41-50.

Клесов И., Лексаков А., Российский С. Вопросы организации зонной обороны при игре «четыре защитника в линию» / И. Клесов, А. Лексаков, С. Российский // Теория и практика футбола. – 2004. – № 4. – С. 2-5.

Колосовский Ю. Совершенствование взаимодействий игроков линии обороны при зонной игре / Ю. Колосовский // «Футбол-Профи». – Донецк (Украина). – 2006. – № 4 (5). – С. 28-37.

Лаверс К. Действия игроков в обороне в ситуации «один в один» / К. Лаверс // В книге: Пособие для футбольных тренеров. – М.: Фонд «Национальная академия футбола, 2007. – С. 250-253.

Люкези М. Футбол. Обучение системе игры 4-3-3 (пер. с англ.) / М. Люкези. – М.: ТВТ Дивизион, 2008. – 164 с.

Морозов С. Анализ зонного метода обороны при игре «в четыре защитника» / С. Морозов // «Футбол-Профи». – Донецк (Украина), 2006. – № 1 (2). – С. 16-19.

Стонкус С. Секреты зонного прессинга / С. Стонкус // Спортивные игры. – 1966. – № 6. – С. 11.

Сурков Е.Н. Антиципация в спорте / Е.Н. Сурков. – М.: Физкультура и спорт, 1982. – 143 с.

Футбол: учебник для ин-тов физ. культуры / Под ред. М.С. Полишкиса и В.А. Выжгина. – М.: Физкультура, образование, наука, 1999. – 253 с.

Чирва Б. Суть и принципиальные отличия тактики действий обороняющегося игрока при персональной опеке, «закрытии зоны» и индивидуальном зонном прессинге / Б. Чирва // Теория и практика футбола. – 2002. – № 1. – С. 2-7.

Чирва Б. Величина игрового пространства, которое могут перекрыть футболисты при разном расположении, как предпосылка к выбору тактики игры в обороне / Б. Чирва // Теория и практика футбола. – 2002. – № 3. – С. 2-6.

Чирва Б. Основы зонного прессинга: принцип действий обороняющихся игроков в ситуациях «один против атакующего игрока без мяча» / Б. Чирва // Теория и практика футбола. – 2004. – № 3. – С. 2-9.

Чирва Б. Система игры в обороне команды, применяющей в обороне зонный прессинг и использующей трех защитников и пять полузащитников: расположение игроков при вводе мяча в игру из-за боковой линии в средней зоне поля / Б. Чирва // Теория и практика футбола. – 2004. – № 4. – С. 6-9.

Чирва Б. Двое против атакующего игрока без мяча, находящегося между ними по длине поля / Б. Чирва // «Футбол-Профи». – Донецк (Украина), 2006. – № 2 (3). – С. 26-31.

Чирва Б. Основы зонного прессинга: действия обороняющихся игроков в ситуациях «двое против атакующего игрока без мяча, находящегося перед ними по длине поля» / Б. Чирва // «Футбол-Профи». – Донецк (Украина), 2006. – № 4 (5). – С. 20-27.

Чирва Б.Г. Футбол. Базовые элементы тактики зонного прессинга / Б.Г. Чирва. – М.: ТВТ Дивизион, 2006. – 80 с.

Чирва Б.Г. Организация оборонительных действий в системе зонного прессинга в футболе / Б.Г. Чирва // Вестник Московского университета МВД России. – 2007. – № 5. – С. 162-164.

Чирва Б. Освоение базовых элементов тактики зонного прессинга: обучение умениям контролировать соперника в ситуациях «один против атакующего игрока без мяча» / Б. Чирва // Теория и практика футбола. – 2009. – № 4. – С. 35-38.